JOURNEY INWARD, JOURNEY OUTWARD

JOURNEY INWARD, JOURNEY OUTWARD

Elizabeth O'Connor

1817

HARPER & ROW, PUBLISHERS
NEW YORK, HAGERSTOWN, SAN FRANCISCO, LONDON

Photographs by Hart Cowperthwait

FIRST HARPER & ROW PAPERBACK PUBLISHED IN 1975

ISBN: 0–06–066332–4

LIBRARY OF CONGRESS CATALOG CARD NUMBER: 68–11728

82 83 84 85 86   10 9 8 7

TO

Gordon Cosby

whose gift to others is the exercising

of his own great gift of faith

Contents

PREFACE   ix

1 The Inward Journey   1

2 Three Engagements on the Journey Inward   10

3 Calling Forth of Gifts   28

4 The Restoration Corps   39

5 The Frontier Church and Psychiatry   52

6 The Potter's House   62

7 New and Old Forms of Worship   77

8 Preparation for Mission   101

9 The Covenant Community   115

10 For Love of Children   138

   EPILOGUE   167

   APPENDIX: The Coffee House Church   173

   PICTURE SECTION FOLLOWS PAGE   116

Preface

This book is a continuation of the story which was begun in *Call to Commitment*. It is written in response to those in the churches who have touched the life of this community. They have given us a secure sense of our belonging to the world-wide body of Christians, and stimulated our thinking and encouraged our work. Probably most of all, these friends have helped us by their penetrating questions, which in turn have called forth questions in us.

Out of our dialogue with other churches has come greater awareness of the need to hold in some kind of creative tension the "inward journey" and the "outward journey." It is these two emphases in our congregation which seem to speak to those outside the Church, as well as those who belong to it. It is as though intuitively a person knows that his life is to have these two dimensions.

Those congregations whose stress has been on the inward—worship, small prayer groups, and study programs—are sensing that the call to wholeness involves more than this, while those who have abandoned this part of the inward journey to carve out in the cities the new forms of the church are receiving hints that all is not well with these missions. Perhaps, more than anything else, the story recorded here is a glimpse of our own struggling with what it means to be on both these journeys. Certainly we are convinced that one is shallow and lacks substance without the other. We are going to know little about the task of reconciliation in the world unless we are in touch with what goes on in that world within ourselves and know how difficult reconciliation is there. We cannot begin to cope with what it means to build a world community unless we understand how difficult it is to be in community even with a small group of people, presumably called by their Lord to the same mission. Nor will we know the full power of the Spirit while we cling to our upper rooms.

A book like this is not written without the help of many people. I am especially grateful to those in our mission groups who were eager for me to write of things as I saw them. Along with the congregation of the Church of the Saviour, I am grateful to the people of Seaton Place, who taught us something about what it means to be poor, and were willing to bear with us in our learning. Where I felt they would want it I have changed the names of the people on Seaton Place. We are indebted to the families of FLOC, who probably more than any others awakened us to what white America had done to the Negro in Washington. These families continue to broaden our horizons. With them we are learning that God really is at work in his world. It is not simply popular theology that we can join him in that work. Things do not have to be as they are; laws can be changed and dehumanizing structures overthrown.

I want to thank Alma Newitt, whose editing of this book contributed to the clarity of countless sentences and to any smoothness in these pages. I am also grateful to Ruth Fox, who typed the manuscript with a perceptive and editorial eye.

JOURNEY INWARD,
JOURNEY OUTWARD

I

The Inward Journey

There is an adage which the world gives to us. It says that if we do not look out for ourselves, no one else will. There is more than one meaning for this, and more than one way to say it. It is possible for it to mean that within each of us is a self to be known and cherished—"What will a man gain by winning the whole world, at the cost of his true self?" (Matt. 16:26, NEB) But if the adage once had that meaning, it is lost. It is now used to remind us to hang on to what we have, to be anxious for tomorrow—what we shall eat and what we shall wear. It is used to let us know that no help may be expected from a neighbor. We heard this as children, and now as adults we have in our experience the proof of it; each day the newspapers carry accounts of neighbors who did not respond to the screams of their neighbors. We who would be shaped by Christ are shaped by headlines and the counsel of friends who do not know Him.

I have an accident with my car. The other driver is at fault and is charged. He is sorry and assures me that a representative of his insurance company will come to see me and all will be taken care of. In the interim, my friends advise me to have a lawyer. They tell me I will be tricked into signing papers I do not want to sign. They warn, "You will be asked questions in such a way that your answers make you guilty." I listen to the counsel, and I am caught up in it. I am not practiced in placing my life beside quiet waters where the Spirit of God can brood upon it. The still waters are for moments of crisis. The small happenings I respond to by the counsel of men conformed to the world, but I am acquainted enough with another world to be uneasy. I do not hire a lawyer, but when the company's agent arrives I look upon him as my enemy, and I am perplexed, for something or someone lets me know I was to have greeted him as a brother. He also knows me as *his* enemy. The books of his company bear the records of countless numbers who were out to get all they could. He keeps insisting that I need not expect to get rich on this accident, though I have twice made it clear that I want only the bills taken care of. On an ordinary level there was no opportunity for us to encounter each other as persons. What each of us concluded before we met was that we could not trust the other.

Laurens van der Post in one of his papers reminds us of the legend of the white and black knights at King Arthur's court, which illustrates what our meeting with another often is.

> There were two brothers, the Black Knight and the White Knight, and they set off on a quest, each on his own, one going north and the other one south. After many years they met in a dark wood, and did not know each other. They immediately assumed that they were enemies until, when both were lying bleeding to death on the grass, they undid their helmets and recognized that they were brothers.*

The question is, can the recognition come before the fatal blows are struck? The answer that comes to me is: only if my life is grounded in the God of us both. We do not even have to ask if another will prove himself trustworthy. The question for each of us is, "Am I trustworthy?" Is there within me a strength that lets me be unafraid? Can I allow myself to be present to another because I can trust my response and know that I am able for whatever

* *Inward Light*, Vol. XXVILI, No. 67, p. 37.

comes? All of life puts the same question. Can I be present to it, or have I so little trust in my own inner resources that I am fearful of hurt, fearful of loss, guarding myself—not daring to lose my life, and therefore never finding it.

This being present to another is not something that can be willed. It comes as we experience what it means to be present to ourselves. The essence of it is contained in the scripture: "The kingdom of heaven is within." The transforming power wells up from within—"For my gift will become a spring in the man himself . . ." (John 4). So much of the threat we know comes because we do not really believe this, and are off drinking at wells that serve for a time, but leave us anxious because we so quickly thirst again. And yet the way that leads to loss of real self is the one that most of us are traveling. And Jesus, always the realist, knows this and issues grave warning. "The gate that leads to life is small and the road is narrow, and those who find it are few" (Matt. 7:14).

Often we are not even aware that there are two ways. I can write a book which will employ the tools of the craft to create interest. Its observations will be accurate and properly documented. It will be orderly in design and communicate a message. In the world of books it may even for a season find a place. But there is another way to write a book. There is a book which can come out of the depths of one's self, so that the ordinary is transcended and one is surrendered to the creative force that moves through all things. If I write the first book, I must consider its timeliness, and how many books have been written on the subject, and all that it is proper to weigh when one is competing in a competitive market. If I write the second, I do not have to be concerned about these things or fear that what I do will be outdated. It may be on a subject used a hundred times, but it will be a subject made new. The book will have individuality as a person has individuality.

A creative work always has its own life. The painting that comes out of the life of an artist is not repeatable. Others can be influenced by it, but they cannot copy the essence that makes it what it is. The imprint of the creator is not in the subject or the techniques. This is why the true artist can give freely to another artist all he knows. Because he lives close to the center of his own life, he will not be threatened by the success of another. He knows that it does not rob him of anything that is his own. The work of others can only enlarge his horizons and call forth his own gift. He can stand before the work of other artists and receive into his life a newness that will make him different. So while it is true that one creative work cannot detract from another, it does not follow that it may not add to another. It will change the man who looks with *beholding* eyes.

Sometimes the artist does not remember this. He becomes a critic of the work of others as he grows afraid. It is as though the other were his competitor, or could be, and he has forgotten the mysterious uniting of elements that happens in himself to produce a work. Either this, or he paints in the way of most men, using only observations and techniques and skill. It may, as with the writer, be a very good work, pleasing to the eye, but it is not creative in the profound sense. It has not come from the deep center of himself, where forces within him unite, and something happens which is through him and of him, but which even he cannot cause to happen again. The artist who is operating on the more surface level has reason for his fear. He has many competitors, and they may seek to occupy his place, for after all he is not in his real place, which means that he can be displaced. He is not even in the place of another man, since it is not possible to take a place that truly belongs to another.

No, the place where he is does not belong to any one. One holds it, and then another. It is won by the usual means of aggression, or industry, or cunning, or deceit, or skill, or knowledge, and in these ways it can be lost. This is common practice and there is nothing to be said about the wrong or the right of it. This is not what we are discussing, but the fact that there is another way—one that belongs to an entirely different order of things, whose governing laws are different. The place a man finds under these other laws is really his own, and when he has found it he is not afraid, because there has grown up in him the knowledge that it cannot be taken away. He is in the place that was prepared for him when the foundations of his life were laid.

The artist has been used as an example here, but only to illustrate the general plight. Each of us is the artist of his own life. The materials we are given to work with, the conditions we work under and what happens to us, are part of the drama of what we shall do with our lives. But materials and conditions and events are not, in themselves, the determining factors. Whether a man arrives or does not arrive at his destiny—the place that is peculiarly his—depends on whether or not he finds the Kingdom within and hears the call to wholeness—or holiness, as another might say. The man who hears that call is chosen. He does not have to scramble for a place in the scheme of things. He knows that there is a place which is his and that he can live close to the One who will show it to him. Life becomes his vocation.

To have life as vocation is to be aware that there are two ways to go—the wide road and the narrow road. The wide road might be called the way of unconsciousness and the narrow road the way of consciousness. The wide road is the road of the crowd. Jesus describes the people on it as not seeing and not hearing. They have an invitation to a banquet, but are too busy to attend. They always have something very important that needs to be done, and their reasons are always logical and convincing. They can explain well to others because they have explained well to themselves, silencing any murmurs of dissent that come from within. They have lost awareness that there are two ways. They respond to externals only, since their attention is outward. They have many answers. When they do ask questions they ask them of others but never themselves. There is a sameness about those in the crowd. By contrast with "round characters" that develop and change, they are what in fiction writing is known as "flat characters," which means that they do not change. They are the same at the end of the story as at the beginning. They do not receive anything into themselves; things happen to them, but never in them. Their lives are rich in outer events, and poor in inner ones. They are the impoverished who are not included in any poverty program. They are the dead who do not know they sleep.

There is something comforting about descriptions of the crowd, for it is easy to think that we do not belong to it. Who is there that cannot summon up a few encouraging examples by which to place himself outside its boundaries? I can remember questions that I put to myself one day. I can remember an event that changed my thinking. I can remember a time of decision when I was aware of two roads and chose the narrower. But these are isolated experiences that return as a reminder of a Way that exists. They are not the ways of many hours or many days. In reflection, I grow aware that most of the time I walk with the crowd on that wide and populated highway. I am lost to myself.

The process of becoming lost to oneself can begin in childhood with parents who, because they were not present to themselves, could not be present to their children. Not only do these parents impose upon a child standards and goals that are not his, but they impose upon him what is hidden from their own sight. C. G. Jung writes,

> Generally speaking, all the life which the parents could have lived, but of which they thwarted themselves for artificial motives, is passed on to the children in substitute form. That is to say, the children are driven unconsciously in a direction that is intended to compensate for everything that was left unfulfilled in the lives of their parents. Hence it is that excessively moral-minded parents have what are called "unmoral" children, or an irresponsible wastrel of father has a son with a positively morbid amount of ambition, and so on.*

The parent, instead of calling forth the individuality of the child and nurturing in him an awareness of his own unique destiny, makes the child an extension of himself. There is no separateness. This in itself creates anxiety, for even the child lost in the parent and the parent lost in the child know at the deepest level of their beings that a precious coin has rolled away. The anguish becomes acute for the adolescent trying to discover and be himself, and needing to belong. If he doesn't melt into the teen-age gang and accept whatever may be the current vogue, then his peers, the crowd of his age, make it clear that he is a "square." Even parents who know about the narrow gate begin to think of surrender to the values of the group. They cannot let their children bear the pressures of alienation. No support comes from the schools, since their concern is not the preservation of individuality but the education

---

* C. G. Jung, *The Development of Personality, Collected Works* Vol. 17 (New York: Pantheon Books, 1954), p. 191.

of the masses. No support comes from the churches, for the churches have forgotten that the concerns of Christianity are for the individual, and are preoccupied with numbers.

The child so easy to mold, the adolescent so anxious to conform, becomes the adult shaped from without instead of from within. In whatever way it happens, the person who has lost his true self has a hunger in him. It may be expressed in apathy or in industry. He may try to satisfy it with a job he works at fourteen hours a day, or a family that is "everything" to him, or success that is worth all striving, or the acquisition of things, of which there is no end of wanting. But there is nothing to fill the emptiness of the one who is not following the way of his own inner being. A fear begins in him. Something lets him know that he is missing out. He looks at the crowd, and it seems to him that it is passing him by. He is of the crowd, but no one there acknowledges him. The faces are blurred. As this one and that one go by, he may even reach out to touch and know, but then things happen inside him. Jealousy and envy spring up. He wonders if that other might not be in his place, or have what he needs. He cannot be sure who is friend and who is enemy. He begins to assign thoughts to the other that the other is not thinking, or responses he is not making. He cannot call the other into presence, because he himself does not know presence. He has no confirmation from within, and therefore must seek it in the other, which means that he cannot be present to the other as the person he is. He goes forth to meet the other, but then he begins to wonder, "Will I say the right words, make the right impression, do the right thing?" Or the meeting may be interrupted by an entirely different set of feelings. "How will the other serve my ends?" "What does he want of me?" Or perhaps it is the look of the other that cancels out the intended meeting—the accent, the color, the dress, a mannerism or way of speaking.

In the crowd no one is responsible. All are innocent. No one is in violation of the commandment to love the neighbor, for no one even sees the neighbor.

Does this, then, raise for those in the crowd the question of how to step out of the crowd, how to recover the lost self? No. "What must I do to be saved?" implies that one knows he is lost. It says that one is acquainted with his own pain. It indicates awareness of being on the road which Scripture says "leads to destruction." But this state has the whisper of consciousness. It is removed from unconsciousness, which is the mark of the crowd.

Are we to believe, then, that there is no way to step out of the crowd? Not so. While it is true that all things conspire against it, God conspires for it. There comes an event, or a flash of insight, or a demanding ache. There comes a person who is in the crowd, but not of it. These are moments God uses to put in the heart and the mouth the question, "Is there another way?" When that question is asked, one can begin to hear about the inward journey, or the "narrow gate." But from learning that there are two ways— one that leads to death and one to life—it does not follow that we enter by the narrow gate. The facts about that gate are starkly simple.

> One, it leads to life, but
> Two, it is a hard way, and
> Three, few find it.

For those who would be on the inward journey, these are three facts to ponder at the beginning and end of each day. We must cling to the first against temptations, and false prophets, and glittering goals. We must hold to the second lest we be too easily turned aside or corrupted by the illusion that something can be had for nothing. It is part of our sickness that we go after the high prize with so little understanding of the cost and so poorly equipped to meet and withstand the armies that will do battle against us. We do not ask for courage, because we do not know we have need of it. We are given over into the hands of the enemy without having discerned his shape on the horizon.

The man who would step out of the crowd and follow his own destiny, must keep before him the knowledge that the way is hard. But even if he is aware of this, he is still in danger. He must remember, also, that few find it. It will grow easy for him to imagine that he is on the way when he is not. This is where the religious lose out on the Kingdom. They assume that because they are aware of the two ways, and because they have chosen the second, they are on it. This is to fall comfortably into the sleep of the crowd again. It may well be a "religious" crowd, but it is nonetheless a crowd.

This is a book about the "narrow gate," which will henceforth be referred to as the inward journey. It is a book concerned with the renewal of the church, for it holds that renewal cannot come to the church unless its people are on an inward journey. It holds with equal emphasis that renewal cannot come to the church unless its people are on an outward journey. The outward journey is not to be confused with the way of the crowd. Those on an outward journey can see the neighbor. Their world includes the technological age, the modern metropolis. They are concerned with shaping the church for responsible involvement. While it is a crucial mistake to assume that churches can be on an outward journey without being on an inward one, it is equally disastrous to assume that one can make the journey inward without taking the journey outward. So this is also a book about the outward journey and a church's struggle to contain both movements within its life.

2

Three Engagements on the Journey Inward

"Inward journey" and "outward journey" are familiar terms in our community. We use them to describe what the Christian life is all about. We use them to describe the meaning of membership in the Church of the Saviour. As a community of faith we are committed to being a people on an inward journey and a people on an outward journey.

The inward journey involves us in three engagements. These Gordon Cosby* has held before the community since its founding. Not only are they subjects of sermons, but the whole of the church's life is structured to make them possible.

The first engagement is with oneself. We have come increasingly to see the need of consciously moving toward self-knowledge. We had some understanding of the injunction of the ancients to "know thyself" and the writings of depth psychology about the vast unconscious in each of us, but more than this was necessary to begin

* Minister of the Church of the Saviour, Washington, D.C.

with any seriousness a journey into self. We needed the collaboration of our own experience in a community to understand that self examination was essential, if we were to have a life together and to be in any meaningful way the Church in the world.

It is easy for the religious to become closed and unyielding when this dimension of the spiritual life is absent. These are the religious who never seem real. With them you never feel up against something which has substance—the word become flesh. One wonders whether this may not be a large factor in the current rebellion in Protestantism against the life of devotion. Are the reformers who say we need new symbols and new vocabularies to communicate with those outside the church projecting onto the world their own emotionally charged reactions against a religious fare in childhood which did not feed their real hunger? In our own community the previously unchurched often seem more tolerant and open to different types of religious temperament than those with a religious background who have adverse feelings triggered by a word, or a statement, or a line in a bulletin. I remember one visitor on a Sunday morning who asked one of our new-to-the-church people, "Have you been washed in the blood of the Lamb?" Our former worldly man looked at him and said, "I don't know, but if you will wait here, I'll find out." If that visitor had addressed his question to any number of people in our community who have grown up in narrow religious homes, they would have visibly recoiled at his choice of words, walked off, and never returned.

Several years ago I was invited to a conference of ministers who came together at Dayspring to consider what the strategy of the church should be in these revolutionary times. I was invited because of my membership in a church which had pioneered some successful new forms. As a church we held then, as now, the conviction that these forms had grown out of an emphasis on the inward life, but when I mentioned prayer there was a shudder. I began that weekend to observe that many vital and sensitive Christians who are pioneering the new forms of the church have the most difficulty, not only with the church's vocabulary, but with the development of an interior life. One of the participants at that conference gave some explanation out of his own spiritual biography. "I was raised," he said, "in a household where prayer was used to manipulate and restrict life. I had to go through a time of rebellion before I could come to know another kind of prayer, but I still can identify with the feeling inside that makes those who have been raised in the church turn away from religious words and practices. They have been turned off by the unreality in so much of it."

We have to be people engaged with ourselves, if we are going to find out where we are and where it is we want to go. Are we among those who take religious words and tuck them away in shallow places, so that when we use them they offend the truth of others because they do not belong to the truth of our own lives? Or are we the religious grown so sophisticated that we would not be caught dead with an inappropriate word, and view with distaste all who have not arrived at our own advanced position? The fact is that the capacity for either extreme is in each of us, and we move toward wholeness as we face our own prejudices.

I recall a hard and literal-minded woman whom I encountered one night in the coffee house. I felt trapped while I was with her and took the first chance to move out of her company. A month later in a class on modern theological trends I found myself using hostile, defensive words, and I was reminded of that woman because I sounded to myself as she had sounded. I had thought that a great gulf separated us, but since that meeting with her I have seen some of the places where the walls of my own life are up to keep out what is unknown and threatening. They may not be positioned where hers are, but the fact is that they are there, and they close out and wall in.

Esther Harding in her book *The 'I' and the 'Not-I'* illustrates our limited awareness of the world within and the world without.* She writes that biologists, studying the nature of consciousness in animals, have found that each creature sees and hears only what concerns itself and is insensitive to all else. She further states that each animal lives in a world of its own, an *Umwelt* or enclosing world which consists only of those objects in the outer world to which it responds.

One of Dr. Harding's vivid examples is the "world outlook" of

* M. Esther Harding, *The 'I' and the 'Not-I'* (New York: Pantheon Books, 1965), pp. 17-18.

the wood tick, who at certain times in its cycle needs the blood of warm-blooded animals for reproductive purposes. At this stage the wood tick will attach itself to the bark of a tree and wait for its victim to pass. There are many ticks in the forest, and few warm-blooded animals, and the wait has been known to be as long as seventeen years. During this time there is nothing else that meets the need of the tick, and there is nothing else to which it responds. While consciousness grows, the higher we go in the animal world, man still lives in a very limited *Umwelt*. Dr. Harding emphasizes that the *Umwelt* theory applies to the human being not only in regard to his physical environment but also the psychological environment in which he lives. Each of us, like the wood tick, tends to see only what concerns us or meets our need, and to be blind to everything else. We are not conscious of what is around us or within us. The life task of each person is to enlarge his own narrow *Umwelt,* or to grow in awareness—"Awake, O sleeper, and Christ will give you light."

As people on an inward journey we are committed to growing in consciousness, to becoming people in touch with our real selves, so that we know not only what flows at the surface, but what goes on in the depths of us.

Part of this engagement with self will be the asking of questions. It is strange that the climate of the church so often has not permitted asking questions, when it ought to be known as a place for the calling forth of questions. In the Parsifal story, the hero's years of wandering are necessary because when, as a young man, he accidentally found the Grail castle, he could not understand it and therefore was unable to ask the right question about its meaning. This points up the fact that it is not just questions that we need to ask, but the right ones. As members of the church, we need to resist the temptation to give answers to questions that no one has asked, and deal with that in ourselves which prevents us from creating an atmosphere in which we and others can question. And the teacher, whoever he is, ought not to be a man of answers but a man of questions. "Who do men say that I am? Who do you say that I am?"

We need to ask questions, and most of these we need to address to ourselves. "What made me respond as I did? What is the reason for my depression? Why is there this unrest in me?" These are some of the questions that the psalmist asks in his engagement with self:

> Why are you cast down, O my soul,
>   and why are you disquieted within me?
>   Ps. 42:5, RSV

Having put our question to ourselves, we need to trust the answers that come from within, so that we are not always demanding from others what must be discovered by tilling and tending the soil of our own lives. There may be a morbid kind of introspection, but there is also an introspection necessary to growth, or we crystalize at a given point and become rigid and unchanging. Each of our years is to be richer than the one before, so that the end of life finds us living in a vastly expanded *Umwelt,* seeing a world we could not have imagined in youth. Flexibility and openness to life should be the hard-won marks of the old. Instead, the opposite is more often true. The walls close in and restrict, and age is not embraced or celebrated. Advertisements and TV commercials play on the anxiety that the thought of old age engenders in us. We accuse mass media of making us into a society of youth worshipers, when it simply fosters our own idolatry. The mantle of youth deludes us about the future. It blinds us to the fact that tomorrow is determined by today. It is now that the young decide what they will be like in middle age and old age. We are under the illusion that rigidity and narrowing of life only begin in age, when actually they begin in the twenties or thirties or whenever we abandon the the journey inward; and like any progressive disease, they become more evident with years. The church needs to remind us that we do not evade forever the One who knows how to ask questions.

> Oh, my soul, be prepared for the coming of the Stranger,
> Be prepared for him who knows how to ask questions.*

Our dreams can help us in that preparation, for they are a rich source of self-knowledge. They hold messages which can bring us

---

* T. S. Eliot, *Choruses From "The Rock,"* Collected Poems, 1909-1962 (New York: Harcourt, Brace & World, Inc., 1930), p. 192. Used by permission of Harcourt, Brace & World, Inc., and of Faber and Faber Limited, London.

close to our own truth. They can speak to us of what has been lost to conscious memory. Or they can throw new light on the present, so that the way we look at someone or respond to something is fundamentally changed. Or dreams can make us aware of a part of ourselves we have denied, which wants to be heard.

Always man has known that dreams were important to him and has pondered their meaning. Through the centuries are found tales of his efforts to be instructed by dreams. The Bible from beginning to end abounds in stories of dreamers and their dreams. For Jesus a dream was a matter of life, and a dream was a matter of death: it was Joseph's heeding of a dream that let Jesus escape those who sought His life, and it was Pilate's failure to give attention to another that delivered Him to death.

It is probably only since the advent of psychoanalysis, which fully established the significance of dreams, that we have ceased to give them the same attention. One might have expected that we would become more ardent students of our dreams, but instead this seems to have convinced us that they are the province of the professional interpreter. While science and the laboratory give us a vast amount of new information on dreaming, it has no meaning for our individual lives.

If it is true—and few men of learning dispute it—that our dreams reveal profound aspects of ourselves, then they become the concern of every man, not only of the specialist and those who can afford his services. This is not to put aside the complexity of dream interpretation, or to suggest that we can go back and approach them with the superstition and conjecture of dawning civilizations. We can neither take our dreams literally, nor buy a book on symbols and make a parlor game of them. But we can give attention to what modern psychology is saying about dreams, and we can dare to meditate upon our own dreams. To fail in this may be to find ourselves, for all the riches of our scientific age, poorer than ancient man, who engaged in the struggle to understand the meaning of a dream for his life.

C. G. Jung gives encouragement. "I share all my readers' prejudice against dream interpretation as being the quintessence of uncertainty and arbitrariness. But on the other hand, I know that if we meditate on a dream sufficiently long and thoroughly—if we take it about with us and turn it over and over—something almost always comes of it."* Jung did not feel that this "something" was such that one could boast of its scientific nature, but he did believe it would be a practical and important hint which would show the dreamer the direction in which his unconscious was leading him.

There are many ways to be engaged with self. Certainly it is important to observe that our lives are fragmented. Bonhoeffer, in his *Letters and Papers from Prison*, points out that the Scripture verse, "Ye therefore shall be perfect as your heavenly father is perfect" (Matt. 5:48) is properly translated "Ye therefore shall be whole [or complete] as your heavenly father is whole," and contrasts this with the double-mindedness of James 1:8. Jesus in his priestly prayer asks the Father that "they may be one, as we are one," but most of us glimpse only for fleeting moments, if at all, that we are divided. We fail to recognize ambivalent feelings and conflicting thoughts and contradictory acts. One part of us goes through the ritual of making resolutions which another part has no intention of keeping, but we are none the wiser when we fail and try again. We make no effort to study the opposing forces so that we know what they are and can consider their weapons. Instead we explain our failures with some general statement that is usually a commentary on lack of will power. In this way our own lives continue to be battlefields where ignorant armies clash by night.

Recognition of the division in ourselves begins when we shift the attention we have been giving to the mote in our brother's eye and fasten it on the beam in our own. In an age, however, when so many suffer because they feel no sense of self-worth, it is equally important to become aware of the light in us—that part of us which is based on truth. Light and dark—they are both there, and each has many children, the children of darkness and the children of light. "My name is Legion" is the plight of us all.

The second engagement is with God. Whereas no one can know God who does not know himself, it does not follow that knowledge of self is knowledge of God. God speaks through the self, but He is not the self. He can come to us through the revelations of the unconscious, but He is not the unconscious.

St. Teresa of Avila, writing in the sixteenth century, probably

* *Psychological Reflections, A Jung Anthology* (New York: Pantheon Books, 1953), p. 65.

saw as vividly as any the necessity of keeping the two engagements in proper balance. Always with her instructions on prayer she urged the cultivation of self-knowledge. She considered it to be the wiles of the Devil himself that prevented souls from learning to know themselves, and warned her nuns that no soul could be so far advanced that it did not have to study self. "Self-knowledge is so important that, even if you were raised right up to the heavens, I should like you never to relax your cultivation of it."* But she was conscious of what we do not remember when we turn to any concentrated study of self, and this is that it is by God's design that we make the study. Also, that there can be too much of a good thing, which we are most apt to forget when we are new to this kind of study and begin to experience the riches of it. If we have neglected this aspect of the inward journey, then in the beginning of self-study we shall probably have no choice but to give it a preponderance of attention. The important thing to keep in mind is that if we are really to know our own life, we will have to emerge now and then from study of self and meditate on the "greatness and majesty" of God. "As I see it," said St. Teresa, "we shall never succeed in knowing ourselves unless we seek to know God."

This God with whom we will be engaged for the rest of our days comes to us across a great distance, and at the same time He is the divine force at the core of our own lives. He is a God whom we will know in many ways, but one of the primary ways is prayer grounded in Scripture. As people on an inward-outward journey, we are committed to taking whatever time is needed to develop an interior life—a life of prayer. We will take the time to learn how to settle into the silence that is always there. We will take the time to be with God in the quiet places of our spirit, so that we can come to know a different quality of life.

The chorus of voices is growing which maintains that the whole of life is prayer, and that it is artificial to set aside specific times. This leaves unanswered the question of how one arrives at the place where his whole life is the kind of prayer one would have it. What will make us open to being addressed by God in the events

* St. Teresa of Avila, "Interior Castle" (New York: Doubleday Image Book, 1961), p. 38.

of life, to hearing His Word in newspaper headlines and committee meetings, from the careless friend and the impatient clerk? What will keep us from being caught up in the noise and competition and salesmanship in the midst of which we spend most of our waking days? Is it not precisely because God does address us in the arena of life that we must prepare ourselves to hear Him there?

The other night a friend and I had the simple assignment of taking pictures at The Potter's House. We needed a postcard which would capture the atmosphere of the coffee house when lights are low and people are talking by candlelight. Since we could not ask our customers to pose for the necessary time exposure, we had a special photographic party on a night when we were closed, and invited our own people. Our guests could talk and drink coffee, but when we said, "Hold it!" they were to freeze in place for eight seconds. Everyone responded graciously to instructions, although good conversation was interrupted. But even with all this cooperation, everything went wrong. We had made ourselves responsible for too many things, and in addition were working with new and untried equipment. When we had difficulty loading the film and time was slipping away, we became hurried and anxious. Mistakes were made and film wasted. As we asked people to sit again for the same shots we became more hurried and burdened with the feeling of imposing on our subjects. One thing added to another until all calm was gone. We still have no postcard picture of The Potter's House, but there are two people who understand better how easy it is, even in small matters, to be distracted and hurried.

For most of us the days are not filled with events that we label "important." The content and quality of our lives is determined by how we respond to the ordinary, and this depends on whether or not we have taken the time to nourish an inner life. The more pressed we are for time the more essential it is to make recollection a part of our day. There is a profound sense in which our whole life is prayer, whether we strive for it or not, so that much of what we wail and complain about is an answer to requests we are not conscious of making. If we take with any seriousness the idea that our whole life is prayer, surely we will want solitude to meditate on what our posture, and attitudes and acts, are really petitioning.

The person on an inward journey in the church come-of-age will be familiar with all forms of prayer from a simple petition and intercession to meditation and contemplation and the prayer of silence. He will take time to experience a life that is different from his life, and to see a world that is not visible to the ordinary glance. He will know in himself that living word "piercing to the division of soul and spirit, of joints and marrow, and discerning the thoughts and intentions of the heart" (Heb. 4:12, RSV). He will learn that we all possess a charisma of the inner self, which is not extraneous or foreign, but infused into us and made complete by being brought out.

One of the ways for this to happen is to live with Holy Scripture and the men of faith who walk through Scripture. Here the biographer can teach us something about meditation, for the disciplines of a biographer require that he become steeped in his subject. Virginia Woolf spoke of having to be "flooded with the idea" or to "become the person." This sometimes requires years of research, following every available clue, reading pages of written material, maybe traveling to distant places. But then the testimony of every biographer is that one day something happens in him. It is not that he has accumulated enough material to feel that he is a competent reporter of another's life, but rather that he has indeed experienced that life in his own being—or, as Aileen Pippett noted, has "been in some strange way in living contact with the past." She wrote,

> You go into a great man's room and there he is in his accustomed chair; you look through his window and see with his eyes. You catch him making some habitual, unconscious gesture which a portrait painter recorded long ago. You may feel his fatigue in your bones or be refreshed in spirit by the the intensity of his purpose. The illusion will fade, but the conviction that what you glimpsed was real will persist.*

You read those lines and wonder if you could have the same experience if your devotion were equal and your subject were Jesus of Nazareth. Certainly Søren Kierkegaard knew that kind of

* The "Art of Leading a Double Life," *New York Times Book Review,* Aug. 28, 1959.

identity with Abraham, for in *Fear and Trembling* is recorded the journey he took with Abraham and Isaac to the land of Moriah and to the place of sacrifice. He lives his way into history and makes that history his own. This does not mean that he simply takes over the faith of his fathers, but through them he learns of God and experiences not only the Church visible, but the Church spread out in time and space. If we can live with the men and women of the Old and New Covenant deeply enough to hear the Word that God addresses to them, we may come to believe that there is His Word for the journey each of us is to take. For that journey there will be no stakes put out, no guides from the past. When we set out on it we take our place in the line of Abraham and Isaac and Jacob and all those who walk by faith.

One of the ways to begin on this phase of the inward journey might be to take a book of the Bible and live with it for a year. D. T. Niles says that this is one of the practices that he is engaged in for his adult life. Inspired by Dr. Niles, Gordon Cosby began his practice of this discipline with the Book of Psalms.

There are books on the psalms which in the manner of the biographer we can search out and pore over and study. And there are the psalms themselves. Gordon Cosby's way was to learn one psalm a week. First, he went through and read all hundred and fifty psalms twice, checking those that spoke to him at the time, for he knew that unless they had immediate meaning they would be difficult to memorize. By the time he had read them twice, he had checked thirty or forty psalms. These he would glance through each week, and the one that attracted him most was the one he would work on that week. He found that he could memorize it in half the time it took if he just chose one at random. The interesting thing was that later, when he went back and read them all again, those that had said nothing to him the first time often stood out. He also found that it was important to go back each week and review the psalms he had memorized in earlier weeks, or they would be lost to memory.

By the end of the year about a third of the psalms were really in his possession. They were psalms in different categories. He drew upon psalms of repentance when he did not feel repentant, and found—amazingly—that repentance was often stirred in him.

Then there were those of praise, and those that spoke of God being our security. "You use these psalms," he said, "and you begin to really feel that you are kept by God. You go over and over again 'The heavens are telling the glory of God, the firmament proclaims his handiwork,' and the first thing you know you look at the heavens and they are telling the Glory of God. Before, you looked at them and they were just heavens." Bit by bit the experience of the psalmist became his, so that the words were not being merely recited but rose spontaneously to express what he was feeling.

There came a number of times when he wanted to quit and take up the next thing, but he was able to stay with the discipline through the periods when he lost interest. This is important to note, because nothing warrants the name discipline which does not evoke resistance, which means an opposing force comes into action. It is a force which has the potential of sweeping out of sight any good intentions. This is another time to name the enemy and to define the goal. If the discipline is real there will be a goal, for disciplines should not exist for their own sake. Their only value is that they enable us to get to the place where we want to go. They are quite useless if they are not related to our goals. It is, of course, equally foolish to have goals and no disciplines. The goal we have been speaking of here is the one of getting our lives rooted in God, so that they are not blown and tossed about by every wind. We need the engagement with self to find out that we have our houses resting on sand, but there is no possibility of getting them over on rock without an engagement with God.

One of Baron von Hügel's disciplines was to give fifteen minutes each day to devotional reading. He wrote, "Of course such 'reading' is hardly reading in the ordinary sense at all. As well could you call the letting a very slowly dissolving lozenge melt imperceptibly in your mouth, eating." He also wrote, "That daily quarter of an hour for now forty years or more, I am sure has been one of the great sustenances and sources of calm for my life."* When I read this it had immediate meaning for me, perhaps because I tend

---

* *Spiritual Counsel and Letters of Baron Friedrich von Hügel* (New York: Harper & Row, 1964), p. 24.

to fly through books in a compulsive kind of way, which I have come to know is quite useless. Behind me is the experience of reading a hundred books I thought were great, life-changing books that were utterly important for everyone to read. If you mention them now, I can hardly remember what they said, and have no feeling that I am different for having read them. Von Hügel's devotional reading was usually the Bible, St. Augustine's *Confessions,* and *The Imitation of Christ* by Thomas à Kempis.

For my own practice of this discipline I use any book, religious or secular, which is concerned with the three engagements. When I come to a line or thought which evokes a response in me, I stop and meditate on it. Sometimes I simply try to find out what it really means. At other times, when the meaning seems quite clear and I feel I have stumbled on wisdom, I pause to give it an opportunity to take root in me. Then there are times when I follow the train of thoughts stimulated by the reading and arrive at something far away from the original intention of the words. These are times when I collect my own thoughts and opinions, which is more rewarding than collecting the thoughts and opinions of others. The Spirit instructs in this kind of reading, which is important to remember when most of your reading has been done without the benefit of that Spirit.

We need spiritual exercises if we are going to deepen our knowledge of God, but they must be our own exercises. The person who has done quiet, thoughtful, meditative reading all his life does not need von Hügel's discipline. It would be much too easy and offer no opportunity for growth. At least once a year we need to take time to reflect on where we are and what our goals are, and then decide on the disciplines that will help us reach them.

Also, we need to study the forces which will be mobilized against our reaching any of our goals. P. D. Ouspensky in his book *In Search of the Miraculous* quotes an allegory which he says can be found in Eastern teachings and in various forms in many of the parables in the Gospels.

... in one teaching, man is compared to a house in which there is a multitude of servants but no master and no steward. The servants have all forgotten their duties; no one wants to do what he ought; everyone tries to be master, if only for a moment; and, in this kind of disorder, the house is threatened with grave danger. The only chance of salvation is for a group of the more sensible servants to meet together and elect a temporary steward, that is, a deputy steward. This deputy steward can then put the other servants in their places and make each do his own work: the cook in the kitchen, the coachman in the stables, the gardener in the garden, and so on. In this way the "house" can be got ready for the arrival of the real steward who will, in his turn, prepare it for the arrival of the master.*

After we have decided on our goals and disciplines, it might be helpful to name the servants in our own house who have other interests and aims. We need to be aware of these misplaced guides who are trying to manage our household and wrest control of it from the real self who can prepare for the coming of the Stranger. I recently told this allegory to a young man who wanted to keep a discipline of prayer and was having difficulty. I suggested that he name the servants in him who did not want to pray, find out what fear motivated each, and what argument or line of reasoning each presented.

He was able to name four different servants, which he called "four different selves" or the "*A, B, C, D* of my ego." *A* was the practical or skeptical servant, based on the fear that "either there is no God, or my concept and comprehension of Him are wrong. If I really tried to pray I might find that God is not what I think He is." The rationale of this servant was, "Since my comprehension of God is inadequate, it is better to read the thoughts of spiritual masters than to try to pray and experience God in person."

Then there was *B,* the competing servant, who saw life as a race, a competition with all other persons. This servant operated on the fear that if he prayed he would fall behind in the race. His rationale was, "There is a world of work to do, and a crying need for doers. There isn't a moment to lose." This servant would also say, "The circumstances and problems of my life just do not leave me the possibility of prayer."

* New York: Harcourt, Brace & World, Inc., 1949, p. 60.

Another articulate fellow was *C,* the anxious servant, who was fearful that he would fail at prayer. His argument was always, "I'm not a disciplined person anyway. A daily commitment to pray at a set time works for a while, but then I have to rebel against it, so why do it at all? I'll never get to where the masters of prayer are, so better not try."

Another servant he found showing up to run things was *D,* the sophisticated guy whose fear was that he might be fooling himself. "I am afraid my prayer would be baseless and pointless self-delusion." The convincing rationale of this servant was, "I simply don't know how to pray."

Understanding the multiplicity of our being is important for self-knowledge, but it is also important for the engagement with God and with others.

The third aspect of the inward journey is the engagement with others. This is bound up with our whole concept of the church as a people committed to God in Jesus Christ and to one another. Gordon Cosby has said of commitment:

> It says to a specific group of people that I am willing to be with you. I am willing to belong to you, I am willing to be the people of God with you. This is never a tentative commitment that I can withdraw from. It is a commitment to a group of miserable, faltering sinners who make with me a covenant to live in depth until we see in each other the mystery of Christ himself and until in these relationships we come to know ourselves as belonging to the Body of Christ.

Engagement with others in depth is always difficult within the church, which is probably why so few try it and why there is so little genuine Christian community in the world. In other groupings we choose those we want to be close to and those whom we want to hold at a distance, which means that any relationship in depth is on the basis of human affinity and the standards set for friendship. The church is the only place where this does not happen. A person is not received into the membership of the church because he is a certain type or because he has arrived at a certain place in life, but because he can say Christ is Lord. We do not do the calling. Christ does the calling, and this is very threatening if we belong to his Church, because the people he calls are the people with whom we are to have intimate belonging. This gives us a strange assortment of people to be with. They are often not our idea of the ones God should be using to proclaim his Kingdom. Even when we finally get hold of what the Church is all about, we struggle for a long time with pride. At the Church of the Saviour we are aware of this when Christian brethren visit from other churches and ask to meet the members, like people asking to meet spiritual heroes. Under the pressure of wanting to live up to their expectations, we confess our feeling is often "Someone, quick, hide the rolls!"

Whereas Christian community is the most difficult to be involved in, it is the most rewarding and the most essential to those on an inward journey. As we grow in depth relationship with those whose values and experiences are different from ours, the horizons of our little worlds are pushed back—our *Umwelts* are enlarged. Life comes to have a variety and a richness that was not there before.

In this strange community where commitment is not tentative we become free to act and to speak. We can take risks that we could not take in other situations, which include the risk of getting in touch with our own unfelt feelings. We can afford to express negative reactions and move toward meeting, if we know our words do not cut us off. We can choose to express anger and therefore keep the sun from setting on it. We can take the risk of telling a brother what stands between us, if we know there will be another time when we are together, and that it does not depend on what does or does not happen in this moment.

As for those who irritate us and make us always want to get out of their way, they may be precisely the ones who have the most to tell us about ourselves. Modern psychology teaches that what we object to in others is often what can be found in ourselves. We project onto the other what is in us. Esther Harding writes that not only do we live in our own limited world, but our *Umwelts* are "bounded by a transparent barrier separating one from the outside; like glass, it is also a reflecting surface on which one sees one's own image, while of course one thinks that what one sees is the outer world. Consequently, one judges everyone else by one's own standard and from one's own standpoint."*

To the extent that a community has a continuing life together

* *Op cit.*, p. 25.

we are going to be challenged at the point of our illusions about the kind of people we are. This does not mean that we intentionally seek to break the images of others. The task is always to change ourselves—to deal with that in us which prevents our going forth to meet the other. It is when we are locked in a permanent kind of relationship, however, that the conflicts arise which confront us with ourselves. Peace is not the object of Christian fellowship, though we have thought it was and have maintained "good" relationships at the terrible expense of not being real with each other. When this happens, we forego being a people on a pilgrimage together.

A recent book describes the Institute for the Harmonious Development of Man in France, founded by Georges Gurdjieff to awaken students to the inner life.* One of the people at the School was a Russian by the name of Rachmilevitch. Rachmilevitch was a troublemaker and a constant source of irritation to the community. He complained about everything and often threatened to leave when things were more than he could bear. One day he carried out his threat and went to Paris. This should have been an enormous relief to Gurdjieff, but to everyone's amazement Gurdjieff went to great effort to persuade him to return. His explanation was that he needed Rachmilevitch to stir others up. "I know no one person like him . . . who just by existence, without conscious effort, produces friction in all people around him."

Gurdjieff operated on the theory that it was necessary to see oneself without illusion and that friction brought about conflicts in people which shocked them into seeing themselves. I am reminded of this story because the Christian community does not have to import its Rachmilevitches. God gives more than one to each person who comes within the New Covenant.

As we will be severely tempted away from an engagement with God and an engagement with self, so will we be tempted away from an engagement with others. The temptation to withdraw will be at the crisis points in our relationships—at times of real confrontation, and at times when we see nothing happening. And, of course, it will come always at the point of a Rachmilevitch. We will rationalize that it is unprofitable to stick with this particular

* Fritz Peters, *Boyhood with Gurdjieff* (London: Victor Gollancz, 1964).

grouping when there are more congenial people and more congenial circumstances in other places—"people who think the way I
think and feel like I feel"—all of which, when you reflect on it, is
rather dull, and in the second place probably a fiction, since a sure
fact about the next group one joins is that one person there is
certain to be the same—saying the same things, doing the same
things, and evoking the same kind of response. But of course, we
can always move on again when we have settled in enough for the
rough edges of another person to rub against our own rough edges.
We might even be able to withdraw and maintain the illusion that
we still belong to Christ and to his mystical Body, but it will
remain an unconfirmed opinion. The New Testament does not
know very much about this mystical Body. It is concerned with
twelve who have a life together. It talks always about the church at
Corinth or the church at Rome. The answer that is often made to
this is that the Church is wherever two or three gather in His
Name. But this does not only mean the choosing of a few kindred
friends with whom to pray. We gather in that Name when with
other faltering, estranged persons we agree to live a life in depth,
which means learning something about forgiveness and what it
means to be forgiven. It means staying locked in a concrete, given
web of relationships until we come to know ourselves as belonging
to one another and belonging to the Body of Jesus Christ.

It is for these three engagements that the Church must structure
its life. If it can do it without institutions, as some seem to think,
then this is well. If it can't, as others seem to think, then let the
institutions that are raised be tested against whether or not they
make it possible to be on an inward journey.

But the inward journey is not all. There is also the outward
journey.

3

Calling Forth of Gifts

Just as we are committed to being on an inward journey for all of time, so are we committed to being on an outward journey, so that the inner and the outer become related to one another and one has meaning for the other and helps to make the other possible. If this does not happen, then those who are critical of the contemplative man are rightly so. If engagement with ourselves does not push back horizons so that we see neighbors we did not see before, then we need to examine the appointment kept with self. If prayer does not drive us out into some concrete involvement at a point of the world's need, then we must question prayer. If the community of our Christian brothers does not deliver us from false securities and safe opinions and known ways, then we must cry out against that community, for it betrays.

The inner life is not nurtured in order to hug to oneself some secret gain. It is not important in the end that in the quiet of a morning hour we find in ourselves a dwelling place, unless in the midst of the commerce and affairs of men we can get back to it, and what is spoken there and what we become for being there comes to have its influence on the world outside ourselves.

To stand in the silence within oneself, while at the same time relating to external events, is not an easy concept to grasp. It will also be understood differently at different stages of one's life. At twenty, the course of life flows more easily outward. Forty might be the year of balance, and sixty an age when the movement is more inward. Such generalizations can be dangerous, however, since the tides of every life are different, and sometimes at twenty we have been prepared to receive words another cannot hear at forty and may never hear. These are helpful categories only if they teach us reticence, so that we do not burden the young with what they do not hunger for and therefore cannot receive—nor should we burden the old who do not want confrontation with an inner world.

Some never even hear a call sounded—or, hearing the call, they choose not to respond—or responding, do not know how to obey. It used to be the work of the churches to proclaim the Kingdom at hand and then to provide the direction and the structures that nurtured growth in the inner life. But except for rare instances they have forgotten how to do this. In Protestantism it is very difficult to find any help in drawing closer to the real self. If you were searching for a guide on this inward journey and were fortunate enough to discover one in your church or city, his schedule would be so full that he would find it difficult to make an appointment to talk for thirty minutes, let alone enter into a relationship which would exist over any number of years. It might be natural to expect a minister to fill this role, but how many can one serve in this way? Moreover, ministers are given churches when they are yet in their twenties, and those who are older in those churches and might have been their guides on the inward journey often know nothing about it themselves. And the young minister, who has learned in seminary that he is the leader, is not bold to confess in the "congregation of the righteous" that he himself has need of help.

Unless something new and radical intrudes, this generation will continue to equate the inward journey with the ingrownness of much of the devotional life our churches have known. The failure to maintain the tension between inward and outward may account

now for the urgency of the church to be engaged in poverty programs and civil rights demonstrations and community organizations, and its breathless seeking of God at work in the arena of the
secular city. This is not to say that God is not to be found there, or
that the church should not be there. It is the truth of this that has
become terrible to us, and the pain of its knowing breaks here and
there upon the church, sending up a cry to mingle with the prophetic voices of those who say we are the people of the "exodus
God," and the people of the God who is wherever life is "being
ground down." We come late to this truth, and look with dismay
on the religious attitude that saw the world in terms of withdrawal,
fought the intrusion of the scientific, and declared the material
unholy. Dr. Carl Jung says somewhere that "the aspect of themselves which human beings sacrifice in the attainment of a given
object in their lives is reborn alive and comes back after many
years, knife in hand, demanding to sacrifice that which sacrificed
it." Is this not what is happening in the outward movement of the
churches as the emphasis swings from withdrawal to involvement
in the world? Does one not see here and there the knife held over
prayer, over inwardness of life, over the hour of retreat—over God
himself?

The inward must not be sacrificed to the outward, nor the outward to the inward. There is no transformation that way. We who
have houses and goods stored in our barns know that these things
do not give our lives meaning or keep us off tranquilizers, and
when the poor have houses and barns, they will know it too. The
Church will follow the swing of the pendulum back into withdrawal and the myriad substitutes for the religious, and the knife
will be raised again—this time over the outward.

Or is it possible that the hour of our disillusionment, the hour
when there rests upon the Church the imperative to find structures
for involvement in the world, can also be the hour of finding the
inwardness of life, so that in gaining the world the self Christ
speaks of is not lost?

For us the structures to hold the inward and the outward became what we call our mission groups. In these mission groups the
Church of the Saviour finds its shape. Each group has the disciplines essential for the engagement with self and God and others,

and each has those peculiar disciplines for the servant task. In the coffee house one of these disciplines is the simple one of a time commitment. It is not possible to be part of a coffee house mission group unless on one night a week one is consistently on hand between the hours of seven in the evening and one in the morning. If the coffee house is to do its job, it is apparent that these are the hours it must be in operation. It is easy to see what would happen to the mission if the members went home whenever they got tired, or did not come because the day in the office had been too wearing. The disciplines for carrying out the tasks of a mission group do not require explanation. Those who are always shouting "Legalism!" when it comes to the disciplines that concern growth in the inner life will even err on the side of rigidness when it comes to those necessary for the accomplishment of specific jobs. External goals are more understandable because they are evident to our senses—we can see and touch them.

In the formation of mission groups, or cadres, or task groups, as they are called in different places, the inward and the outward are both important considerations, and neither can be ignored with any success. The outward concerns shaping a mission to a need of the world. The eloquent voices of Colin Williams and many others have made this clear, so that we have an understanding which is beyond mere intellectual assent. We are beginning to realize that if the children of the city need a preschool program, then this is a legitimate shape for a church to take; if the city has a need for a place to gather, then a coffee house is a fitting sphere. The renewal of the Church is manifest in the amens which are being said to this. But a lot of frustration has also been engendered. Despite the eagerness of church groups to take the servant form, many of them have been unable to do it in any meaningful way, for it is not enough to say the Church must be shaped by the world's need. This leaves the large and heavy question: Which need? Surveys and studies of surrounding communities have not resolved it, for often agreement cannot be reached on a choice from the multitude of possibilities that exist in every situation. There is juvenile delinquency; there are alcoholism, dope addiction, the aged, the blind, the sick, the broken in mind and spirit; there are slums, with all the problems of housing and education; there are nuclear warfare and the problems of automation and leisure; and on and on runs the list. We can go where the action is, or make some surface decision, but this is not what it means to hear a call or to be "sent." It is only to arrive on the mission field with no word from the Lord.

We are not to superimpose structures on those outside the church, but neither are we to superimpose structures on those inside it. What if one night I wander into a coffee house, and over the months it has meaning for me. I come to know the people who run it, and I ask questions. They tell me about a church, and I come to have an experience that has the sound of theirs, but it is uniquely my experience. I move into the membership of that church and am told that I am needed to wait on tables in that familiar coffee house. I protest that I am no waiter and have no inclination to be one. Then they explain that the Christian life is a sacrificial life, and that my protest is the "old" man in me who will have to be hit over the head many times. I may go dutifully to my post, but no newness will break for another because I am there. Others will not inquire of my life, for they will know intuitively that it has nothing to teach them.

Even in finding its outward shape, the Church must be concerned with its inward pilgrimage. This is the only way the forms can be the real expression of the lives of its people. This is the only way for congregations to be obedient to the command, "Follow me!" This is how the world will hear, "I come that you might have life and have it more abundantly."

In our seeing of Christ as the "man for others" we have swung to another extreme. We look at the structures of the Church and ask, "What do they have to do with the world?"—and come to the conclusion that the life of the Church is ingrown, seeking to increase itself, and that the answer lies in accepting structures dictated by the world, on the terms of the world.

It is true that the structures of the Church have little to do with the need of the world. That is half the problem. The other half is that they so often have little to do with the need of those within a church. They do not help us to realize our essential selves—to follow Christ, who saves us from being other than who we are. The Church has too often told us what to do and failed to help us become who we can be. The new forms of the Church will be shaped by the need of every man to become the person he *can* become. It is our common humanity that we affirm, our need of one another, and above all our sonship—we are joint heirs with Christ. It is the glorious freedom of the sons of God to which all men are called that our structures are to proclaim.

The outward journey is determined in part by the gifts discovered in the inward journey. The story of the buried talents is the story of how seriously God considers the matter of unused gifts. This is what psychiatry calls "unlived" life, which takes its terrible toll—"even that which you have will be taken away." There are a thousand warnings, however, to the man who walks away from himself and his own destiny. Restlessness, sleepless nights, discontent, anger, meaninglessness, boredom—these are the cries of the violated self. Through our suffering we are called back to our own truth: to turn and be healed. We can walk, however, beyond the hearing of the voice that calls, into a land of apathy, complacency, not caring—there is a place beyond the point of safe return. "You will hear and hear, but never understand; you will look and look, but never see" (Matt. 13:14, NEB).

The life of a friend speaks vividly of the importance of listening to one's self. Harvey Moore was brought up by missionary parents, who raised him in the doctrine of service. He had an aptitude for mathematics, and since engineering was an acceptable profession in the society in which he moved, he reasoned that he could serve through being an engineer. He gave himself wholeheartedly to this end, but no peace came to him. "When you are made to feel guilty," he said, "nothing is enough. There is no pleasure in giving. One gives through 'oughtness,' and must strain after new ways to give." This turned him to medicine, because it seemed to him a greater field of service. In preparatory studies, he stumbled on the field of anthropology, and it captured his attention because he wanted to know the "why" of life, but again for the wrong reasons. "Having to justify all I did, I was rationalizing that I would be of even greater service if I could unravel the reason 'why.' I was seeking what is impossible to know. The knowing I wanted would make me God. I began to get intimations that none of the things I had been doing were for me. In trying to penetrate the mystery of the universe, I was banging my head against a wall. There came a day when I was content to wonder at life. As for engineering and medicine, they were not for me, either. Up until then I had been asking, 'What *should* I do?' Now I began to ask, 'What do I *want* to do?' I had always gotten joy out of painting and for the first time I was asking myself what would give me joy. Working with my hands gave me joy. I did not know that I could create with my hands. I just knew that using them gave me pleasure and that this was what I wanted to do."

The pursuit of his own "selfish" ends placed on him a burden of guilt that was to weigh upon him for many years. No one had ever told him that surrender to what is written into the fabric of our lives is surrender to the will of God. Part of him knew it, and this part became strong enough to do battle with the part that did not know, and to take up the cross that every man bears in his becoming.

Harvey doesn't live like middle-class America, and at this moment it is not important to him. He has found the task that is his to do, which is to say that he has heard a call. Whenever this happens, a lot of things which seemed impossible become possible. In response to a call a man can lay down his life. Why is this so? Because he finds his life. The sacrificial life becomes truly worthwhile to him who is discovering the treasure hidden in his own being. He can sell all he has to unearth it. He can gamble and lose. There comes to the "called" man an internal freedom that lets him take the risks involved in following a way. Each day he moves closer to his "true self" and in this comes strength.

Harvey Moore's home, studio, and bronze-casting factory are all in a one-room garage in Georgetown, Washington, D.C. The roof leaks when it rains. There are no carpeted floors, only cement underfoot. The furniture is a desk and bed in one partitioned corner. The rest of the room is working space. Besides long benches, there are two huge furnaces which are the equipment for the "tent-making" that enables him to have free time for the vocation of artist.

Harvey's story does not end with the fact that he has become a recognized sculptor. Only hesitantly should this achievement be mentioned, for the man who is on the journey of becoming fully human does not have to succeed. The adventure is not in the arriving, but in the journey—the "now" of life. When Harvey found a congregation that confirmed him as an artist, and gave to its people the freedom to be, he was able to move back into the life of the Church and to belong to a missionary people; which is to say, a people who provide the structures in which others are free to realize their essential selves. For Harvey, the missionary structure right now is the classes he gives in sculpture at The Potter's House Workshop.

The Potter's House Workshop itself has existed for two reasons that are valid for any mission. First, there is a need in this city for an arts and crafts center where, in a small community of acceptance, people can explore art as an expression of their own lives; and second, because we have had artists in our church who have found the Workshop a challenging vehicle for giving themselves. If we had had musicians, a missionary structure might have been a musical conservatory or a band.

As I write this, those who have been the core members of the Workshop are leaving to pursue their work in new areas, and we are reminded that we must be willing to give up structures not only when they fail to meet a need in the world, but when they no longer provide the framework that lets us be on the "immense journey" of becoming. A call which is valid at one time in a person's life will not necessarily be valid at another time. The young parent may need a structure for his growing and giving entirely different from what he needed as a young single person. The gifts of middle age will have their specialness. The task one is called to in old age will not be that which called us in youth. If we are people on an inward journey, the goal will be more clearly perceived. Also, as we come to know ourselves at new depths, our values and emphases and direction may radically change.

This does not necessarily mean that we misheard earlier calls. It is as we give ourselves unreservedly to what we understand as truth that we come to a new kind of knowing. Maybe we learn with a certainty what is *not* for us, so that we become open to hearing the call which before had only reached us as a muffled sound. This is the call of God in Christ—the call to share in God's mission of reconciliation to His world, which can happen only to the extent that there is a reconciling action going on within us. Webster defines "reconcile" as "to cause to be friendly again." We need to become friendly again toward ourselves, and not to be weighted with guilt by the heretical doctrine that labels the meditative man selfish or self-centered.

The mission-oriented evangelists have cried against the churches huddling in buildings, ministering to their own, but the words do not fit the churches we see. They do not need to be rescued from self-centeredness. They need to discover and nurture the talents in their people that will give them authentic missions.

Wally Wilson is another person in our community who discovered his mission by daring to face the discontent in his own life. This led him to ponder that radical question of what he would like to do. He made a simple discovery. He wanted to cut hair. Contrary to opinion in some places, he felt a haircut made a person feel good. Inflationary prices made him also think that haircutting could be a real ministry to the poor. He was not at all dismayed to find that a barbering course required a thousand hours to complete. We were all better informed on the intricacies of barbering by the time Wally was licensed to cut hair.

Almost two years went by before Wally had opportunity to use his new skill. It came when his work took him to the mountains of North Carolina for seven months of the year. At the little church where he went to worship he met the mountain people, and through them became acquainted with the poverty that surrounded the resort area where he was living. He embarked then on his ministry by helping some of the people paint and fix up their houses. Soon he was using his evenings and weekends barbering and painting. Wally has now been designated as our church's first missionary to the mountain people of North Carolina and authorized to spend his tithe in his work. Part of his assignment is the keeping of a diary and a monthly report to our church on his spiritual disciplines and missionary activities.

In a class in our School of Christian Living, Gordon Cosby was speaking on the subject of Christian vocation. He said in summarizing that the primary task and primary mission of the Christian is to call forth the gifts of others. "We are not sent into the world in order to make people good. We are not sent to encourage them to do their duty. The reason people have resisted the Gospel is that we have gone out to make people good, to help them do their duty, to impose new burdens on them, rather than calling forth the gift which is the essence of the person himself." He then said that we are to let others know that God is for them and that they can "be." "They can be what in their deepest hearts they know that they were intended to be, they can do what they were meant to do. As Christians, we are heralds of these good tidings."

How do we do this? "We begin," Gordon said, "by exercising our own gifts. The person who is having the time of his life doing what he is doing has a way of calling forth the deeps of another. Such a person is Good News. He is not *saying* the good news. He *is* the good news. He is the embodiment of the freedom of the new humanity. The person who exercises his own gift in freedom can allow the Holy Spirit to do in others what He wants to do."

The assignment given the class was for each person to reflect on what his gifts were and to answer the question, "Am I using my gifts?" When the class met again, they were asked to report on the assignment. Only a very few were able to say what his or her gifts were. Others, reflecting hard on what their special gift might be, found no answer. A few, of many talents, said that they had never been able to decide on a particular one, and had dabbled with one thing one year and another the next and never fully developed any. Others able to name a gift felt that it intensified their problem of ego and pride, and they expressed feelings of guilt or vague uneasiness, as though if they really let loose and spent themselves they would be in trouble. Then there were those who rejected the assignment altogether, feeling that it was much too concerned with self. For them there was no relationship between gifts and servanthood. It had never occurred to most of that class, reared in the churches of America, that their servanthood might take a form suitable to their particular individuality. It was not that they were unfamiliar with the emphasis that Christianity puts on personality—the "unrepeatable event" that is a person—but that it had come to them distorted or was mangled in the hearing, so that it always applied to the other person, the person "out there." Even the whole concept of "calling" was difficult to grasp in terms of concrete life. Sure, God "calls." It is not a mistake that the first speech recorded in the Bible's account of mankind is God calling to Adam in the cool of the evening. The Bible story of God calling and God sending is an abstract, biblical concept, quite different from believing that God might call me and might send me. This makes God personal. It means that somehow I count—that it might be possible that within me is the image of God. It might mean that I can be in touch with this calling-sending God.

The discovery of the real self is the way to the treasure hidden in a field. The gift a person brings to another is the gift of himself. Talents are the expression of this self. It is the way the self is sent into the world to use the materials of the world, and to be the bearer of the spirit of God, and—paradoxically—it is the way the self not only remains behind, but is catapulted into the future, for in the creative act the new breaks forth, and the prophetic word is heard.

4

The Restoration Corps

When you live in a community in which the emphasis is on the calling forth of gifts, all kinds of things happen, and you wonder how to keep up with it all. In time you learn that no one does. This is threatening to some—especially to those of us who like to keep a hand on everything. Initially, the church Council, as the governing body of the church, closely supervised the activities of the mission groups. This kind of tight control became less and less possible as new mission groups came into existence. It was difficult enough to follow all that went on in one's own group, let alone a dozen others. There were days when everywhere you listened in, new people were discussing the possibility of mission. Also, the problems in each group were so varied that only those who wrestled with them over long months were in a position to make decisions. It would have been possible to restrict the number of mission groups, but then we could not have been true to the church's calling to let its people express their lives in mission and in accordance with their own unique gifts.

There was also from time to time someone who said we were

becoming fragmented, but this was usually a person not involved in the mission of the church, standing on the sidelines and demanding community. This would not be important to mention, except that from time to time we all stand there. Either we can't find the place where we are supposed to be, or we take ourselves out of the grime and concreteness of a mission for something that sounds better—sounds more spiritual. We forget, if we ever learned it, that our unity is in serving. There is no unity with Christ or his people unless we serve. This is why the exercising of gifts is important. It enables us to serve, to give of ourselves to another. This is how we find out what oneness in Christ is about. When you are moving out in faith to serve another, there comes a oneness within. It makes of your words unifying words and of your deed a unifying deed. There is no Christian community not rooted in service, and no Christian service not rooted in relationship. It is the feet of his friends that Christ washes. Many of us have had to learn this. It was easy to love someone way out there, but the neighbor—the one close at hand—was an altogether different matter.

The story of the Restoration Corps is the story of a half dozen people who discovered a mission and learned to see the neighbor. It began as many of the missions do—around a person exercising a gift. Sharon Avery had been attracted to the church because of its mission program, and yet she finished all the classes without finding a mission she wanted to stay with. She tried The Potter's House and found it wasn't right for her. She hung around the edges of the Workshop, but was never able to move into the center of its life despite a love of color and design. She complained of being miserable and unhappy at home, at work, at church. "I couldn't find a mission," she said, "to call mine, and then someone asked me what I would do, if I could do whatever I wanted. I had a degree in social work, but I had done that enough to know it was not for me. I found the courage to say aloud, 'Interior decorating,' but my question was 'How do you make a mission out of that?' "

No one had the answer, but what the church said to Sharon was, "Why don't you take one of our rooms that needs redoing and work in it?" When Sharon told her husband, he said he would do the painting and invite others to help. About eight people responded to help paint a room, but before they knew it a year was over and they had painted a dozen rooms. To begin with it was just an easy, unstructured, permissive group. There was no commitment of prayer or study or regular attendance. It met on Thursday night and people came or did not come as the spirit moved. "I joined it," said Muriel Lipp, "because I had a large family and did not want to get too involved. It looked like a group where I could get the fellowship I needed and be useful at the same time. Those first weeks everything was fine. We just laughed and argued and painted."

There were times when they did more than laugh and argue and paint. They began to talk about being a mission group and working in the slum areas of Washington. Sharon got excited about helping the poor to decorate their apartments on a little money. When they began to explore this, however, the more experienced told them of other groups who had helped the poor fix their houses only to have the landlords raise the rents. Just at that time they learned that the Federal Housing Administration guarantees long-term, low-interest loans to nonprofit groups for renovating old buildings or putting up new structures. The group began to think of buying a large house, or maybe even a small apartment building, and renovating it with funds secured under Section 221-D3 of the National Housing Act.

While some were eager to move outside the church building, others drew back and began to drag their feet. This was more involvement than they wanted, and yet they had found something in the group which would not let them pull out. It was more than the pressure of a long-term commitment that began to weigh. As they worked on the church, and as they made mistakes, they got close enough to each other to get angry. There was often the accusation that someone was not holding up his end of things. Now they not only painted their way through each room, they battled their way through it. As Sharon got more confidence, she became bolder in her choice of colors. In the pantry she really let go. She was to look back and call it her dark night of the soul. Shocking pink, canary yellow, wedgwood blue, lavender, and orange were her choice of colors. Bravely she mixed them for the group, and obediently they painted, but not without protest. Sharon was certain that when the pantry was completed, she would receive confirmation as an interior decorator. It came from some, but not from all, and she still needed everyone to approve. We all took sides on that pantry. It had been one of those functional, nondescript rooms every large house has, which no one would ever stop to consider twice. Overnight it became the center of a controversy over art, in which we all took a violent either/or position.

Sharon made only one concession to the opposing camp. She gave up the color orange.

The personality conflicts of the Restoration Corps were not confined to its painting activities. As the members became more serious about a mission to the inner city, disciplines and a more structured life became important and raised a whole new set of issues. If they were to be officially approved as a mission of the church, there had to be a core group willing to live its life out in a structure and embrace the disciplines of prayer and worship and study, as well as to involve itself in some segment of the world's life. The subject of disciplines raised the whole subject of authority. There were some in the group who were also in the group therapy program of the church under the direction of Joe Knowles, a trained pastoral counselor. At the mention of disciplines, these members rebelled. They felt that they had been obedient and authority-conscious all their lives. Now, through their participation in the therapy groups, they were learning to shake this, and were not about to submit to anyone's authority.

Every group should have a reconciler, and God gave one to the Restoration Corps in Jamie Eppes. Mahlon Carrington said of himself, "I am always a minority—the hardnosed and cynical one. I don't mean to be negative or obstreperous, but that's the way I sound to everyone." But of Jamie he said, "He knew the King's English. He always said the right thing at the right time. He was with us when we needed him. It was only when we began to shape up that he had to leave for other commitments. It made you think that maybe God had something to do with it."

The Restoration Corps worked through, or battled through, its commitment and was not only authorized as a mission of the church but incorporated under the laws of the District of Columbia as the Community Restoration Corps. Its new status did not enable the members of the corps to dwell in any traditional kind of brotherly love. Hostile feelings were freely expressed in this group. Confrontation was the order of the day. It was not that everybody wanted confrontation. The clash was often between those who felt no true community among persons could exist unless all feelings were openly expressed and examined, and those who were more reserved about their feelings, or felt that things should be kept smooth at all cost. The Restoration Corps was full of extremes. A gay painting party had stretched into agonized months of working through one problem after another. Ground that other groups touched only after years together, this group plodded into with a kind of reckless courage as well as innocence. To the rest of us, "life together" for that little group seemed such a struggle that we wondered why the members kept going week after week.

To each person the reason for hanging on was different. Sharon said, "They gave me the chance to try out the 'new' me. They fought me, but I also knew they were with me." Dennis Avery, the group's moderator, said, "All my life I had been elected to things but I never really believed I had leadership qualities. I didn't believe enough in my own self-worth, which kept me running around doing what everyone else wanted me to do in order to get approval. I wasn't leading. I was counting votes. That kind of thing wasn't going to add up with this group." Don Hardester said, "When we began to talk about a mission in the city, I began to sense a responsibility to something beyond myself. This church has allowed me to make mistakes and do all kinds of things without asking for my qualifications. I began to think I might be able to do this for someone else. I would quit the group and then I would think about it and come back." According to Mahlon Carrington, "It is the longest I have ever belonged to any group or organization in my whole life. I can't stand argument and bickering, and we did plenty of this over small matters, but the difference was, this group managed to argue and get things done. That kept me going when things were rough. Also, I was egotistical enough to think that they needed me."

To be needed is important to the human spirit. It is also important to have a place where one can feel safe enough to walk out in what Sharon called the "new me." It is important to be able to discover what is genuine in oneself and to begin to think in terms of giving and not of getting. Despite all outward appearances, these fundamental and basic changes were taking place in the lives of those who participated in the stormy little group that was now bearer of the promising title "Community Restoration Corps."

They managed, as Mahlon said, to get things done while they argued, and what they discovered as they investigated slum dwellings in Washington was that, of the hundreds they looked at, they were going to have no opportunity to restore any. Section 221-D3 of the National Housing Act might be of aid in other cities, but it was not going to help the poor in Washington. Here even property values in the slum areas had skyrocketed. In addition to purchase cost, the federal housing standards were stiffer than the District government's. These requirements had to be met to qualify for the FHA long-term loan, which meant that renovation costs, together with purchase price, would add up to rent that no low-income family could afford to pay.

The Restoration Corps gave up thinking in terms of help from a federal agency and set out to do what an affluent government could not. Among themselves they raised $2,000. FLOC, another mission of the church, concerned with families whose children were in Junior Village* had found a house that could be purchased for a down payment of $3,500. That mission offered to add $1,500 to the Restoration Corps' $2,000, if the house could be made available to a family with children at Junior Village. As so often happened in the various missions, one mission was able to help the other. The house was purchased. If the pantry had been a dark night of the soul for Sharon, for Muriel it was the purchase of the house. Because of her own small children, she had backed away from the responsibility of personal involvement. It was one thing to help provide a house and another to be in a helping relationship, but the whole program for the families of the children in Junior Village was organized with this in mind. The children were in Junior Village because of inadequate housing, but also because of the emotional instability in their families. "To be a friend to someone needing a friend appealed to me," said Muriel, "but it also frightened me. My greatest despair came in the days before we

* The District of Columbia's institution for homeless children (see Chap. 10).

bought that house. I decided to say Yes to it, but it was the most terrifying thing I had ever done."

The Restoration Corps had lost two members and now numbered six. The purchase of the house was a time when these six renewed their commitment to the mission and to the members of the mission. It was well they did. If the days that led up to the purchase were stormy, they seemed mild to those that immediately followed. With the help of Welfare*, the Restoration Corps had chosen a family to live in the house and had given the Welfare Department a date when it would be finished. I think of Gordon's saying that our mission groups are to be to the world a sign of the Kingdom. That day was not yet for the Restoration Corps. "The neighbors," said Mahlon, "were bound to have heard us. There was never any glamor attached to the Restoration Corps, and now with a deadline some of us were working three and four nights a week. There was trash to be moved out, furniture to be hauled, floors to be scraped, and the whole house to be painted. At the end of every evening, we were dirty and smelly and yelling at each other."

For Mahlon, who was always practical and down-to-earth, the time of testing came when there were just a few days to go and fifteen walls yet to paint and floors to scrape, and he came upon Sharon peacefully painting balloons on the walls of a child's room. There had been dissension for many months between the two of them. It arose over little things like balloons. Mahlon gave balloons no priority. Sharon held them to be essential. Mahlon would come to understand this. One day he would defend Sharon like this, "Her contribution is decorating. She doesn't see floors to scrape, if there is a balloon to paint. It's not that she's intentional about it—she doesn't see this kind of thing. She matches scraps of paint here and there and mixes it up and it comes out looking beautiful. Can I do that? Can you do that?"

One of the miracles of the Restoration Corps was that they learned at a new level of being about the diversity of gifts. They had complained of each other and demanded from each one the same performance on every job. What they came to see was that the gifts were different. One had the gift of working long hours,

* D.C. Dept. of Public Welfare.

another the gift of being a reconciler, another of administrator, another of working with detail, another of handling finances. In the house, there were often jobs like cleaning cabinets that no one seemed to want to do—no one, that is, except Betty Wilkinson; scrubbing a kitchen was joy to her. Also, it developed that she knew about things like plumbing and keeping expense sheets—things you would not expect a girl to care about. As soon as the Corps could, they gave the bank account into her keeping.

As the mission moved into new stages, new gifts were called forth. There was no question that Sharon was the ace, number one "scrounger." The others pitched in to find furniture, but it was Sharon who sensed where the furniture was and ferreted it out. Driving down a street one day, she saw a man standing by a dilapidated chair. She put the brakes on and backed up, and asked him if she could have the chair, though she really didn't want it. She did not even consciously reason that behind that particular chair were better chairs. She simply obeyed an impulse to ask for it. While the man loaded it into the trunk of her car, she told him about the house. It developed that he was a real estate agent with other furniture to place from houses that he was now going to rent unfurnished. From one that had just been vacated he loaded the back of Sharon's car with half-cans of paint and cleaning materials—all they would need. Sharon was to gather in the course of this and other ramblings on back streets a TV set, wall-to-wall carpeting, and a washing machine. In all, the group collected seven rooms of furniture and so many beds they had to give them away.

With each new step the little band discovered a new gift amongst its members, but this did not prevent their biggest blow-up, which came in the last days of working on the house. In the early hours of one morning, after exhausting nights of work, they discussed the job crisis in the family that was to move into the house. A prerequisite from the beginning was that the head of the household be employed. Dennis had reported that the head of the family they had selected with the help of the Welfare Department had been fired that day. The possibility of his securing another job was good, but should they let this family move in with no job? The Corps had already agreed to supplement his earnings by $60 each month, which was a large sum, since the members were already committed to the tithing program of the church. Did they dare risk the possibility of having to pay all the expenses of the family for an indefinite time?

What made the decision more difficult was that Junior Village officials had been given the wrong date for the children to be released, and the week before had delivered seven children to the Welfare Department, which had to return them to the Village. The children had been so upset that two were sick all the way back. These were the youngsters they would disappoint again. Even in the face of the picture of these already hurt children, most of the members said, "We must wait until he has a job." This outraged one member, who protested loudly the inhumanity of it—to which the reply was, "You shouldn't have any voice in it, because you haven't done any of the work." That was the spark that lit the powder. Everyone got into the explosion. Dennis, who was usually quiet-spoken, ended it by four shouted words, "Everyone shut your mouth." Over the months Dennis had come to speak with an authority that welled up from within. A silence fell on the little company and no one broke it. In that silence they put away paint and washed the brushes, and in that silence they left, maybe never to return.

Gordon, in speaking of the responsibilities of a group moderator, always says that one of the primary tasks is to maintain and deepen the unity of the group. If this is to be done, there must be one to continually sound the call. What did he mean by "sound the call"? It was simply the saying again and again what is very elementary—"We are together because of Jesus Christ," or it might be, "This is a mission which God has given to us," or "Christ has first claim on our lives. It is to him we are obedient. We are under his sovereign orders." Proclaiming words which are never said for a group once and for all, but must be repeated over and over again. Perhaps they were different words that Dennis said to each person, but the next day he called each one on the phone and sounded the call, which was a call to do battle not with each other but with the principalities of evil that threatened their unity and the mission which Christ had given to them. When the Corps met again, it made the decision to let the family move in with no job.

It was felt that it would be overwhelming to the family for the whole group to be in relationship with it, so they appointed two of their members to work with the family. Again, it seemed as though they were pairing off opposites in the choice of Don Hardester and Muriel Lipp. Don described himself as projecting onto others either consciously or unconsciously the image of himself as big, loud, and rude, insensitive and profane. It all hid a warm and generous heart acquainted with pain. Muriel was the soul of gentleness, but as Mahlon was to say, "It doesn't pay to underestimate her. She is easy going, but no pushover. This came out after we got the family."

"After the family," "Before the family"—these phrases were to punctuate the conversation of Corps members for months. For them the difference was as marked as A.D. and B.C. They could only speak of their mission in terms of "before we got the family" and "after we got the family." The family came to them as gift. A grace began to mark their lives. When you got close to that group, it was like touching the Church in Acts. Something shiny and wonderful had happened to them. It was not that they were never to argue again, but that somehow with all their individuality, they had become one. Don Hardester described it less biblically, "We are so damned close, it's like being married. I think it's because they are depending on us to be there when they need us."

Don and Muriel first met the mother and father of their family at the Welfare offices. Their sole possessions were seven children in Junior Village and an unpaid-for deep freeze stored in a garage; but to Don and Muriel they were like celebrities. "Seeing them in the flesh," said Muriel, "was like seeing famous people. We had talked about this family for two years, and there they were with real faces and real names. We wanted to speak to them and get to know what they were like inside." That day Don and Muriel took them to see the house. The woman, who was later to speak easily with them, moved silently from place to place; the man, who was not to say very much to them again, commented on every room. Then there came an awkward time when the tour was completed, and they stood in the living room without anything to say to each other. Muriel felt as though they were all fumbling for a way to say thank you, and it was probably in order to take care of moments that were embarrassing to them all that Don said, "Let us pray." They had agreed not to have any religious conversation, and it was certainly understood that they were not to pray. The Restoration Corps was up-to-date on modern evangelism. At the time, the violation of the pact upset Muriel, but she was to look back and know that it was good. They had all needed to say thanks, so why not say it to the appropriate One?

The next day Muriel, with two of her own children, went in a station wagon to pick up their new family. At Junior Village children are separated according to age, which meant that she had to go from building to building to gather the seven. Among the children was much hilarious greeting of each other, as well as sober exchange. In the car the older ones kept passing the baby and the three-year-old back and forth between them. For these two the attention came so late. For too many infant months there had been no one to hold and comfort. Now they had neither smile nor cry, but stayed listless as they were passed from one set of cuddling arms to another. As Muriel drove to the house she stole glances at them, wondering if it was too late to give them back their babyhood. Did the large, unresponsive look in those eyes say that childhood was forever lost?

At the house, the mother hugged each child; the father patted each head, and Muriel left, for there are scenes that tell us we are trespassing.

In the next days the father went to work at a government job, and Sharon came and painted each child's name on a bureau drawer. Once a week Don and Muriel went to visit them. "We never went to see them," said Muriel, "without stopping the car a block away to pray. Their lives had been full of sadness. They had more troubles than one family could handle. I would lie in bed at night and think of them, and wonder how many more there were— out there in the dark—like them, wanting to start over and not being able to because their problems are too overwhelming."

The topic of many of their early conversations was money and how to budget it. They telephoned back and forth on this subject. A budgeted item was a few dollars each week for a credit union at the father's place of work. This the mother would not hear of. Time after time this family had broken up and the children been sent to Junior Village because the father had been on a drinking spree and there had been no money to meet a rent date or buy food, and yet the mother was adamant that no money be put into any kind of savings account. Her answer was simply No. Finally she was able to tell them that it would be no savings account for her—"He'll get drunk and use it." Don was able to convince her that she needed to take the risk of trusting him. The father still gets drunk. Every month the urge to be away and drinking is on him, but thus far he has not touched the money.

"We can't give professional advice," says Muriel. "When we try we are not very good, so we are just friends. This we can be." Muriel had thought her own family would be the greatest handicap to her being in the Restoration Corps, but it became her greatest asset. It quickly gave her a bond with this mother, who turned to her whenever a child was ill or there was a household problem. Many times Muriel would feel herself getting impatient because the mother never seemed to do the obvious things. The children were up until all hours of the night. The household was completely lacking in schedule and routine, and because of this, Muriel began to see that they were not living fully. But she also began to understand it, for over the months she learned that this young mother was also a child of poverty. "She taught me what it means not to have your physical needs met. I had never thought of it. I had always had what I needed."

Don had more rapport with the father, who was afraid of Muriel's "good English." Don did not try to be more than a friend, either. "I had been given freedom to make mistakes," he said. "I could give them that freedom too."

The oldest child in this family had asthma and several times in those first months had to be rushed to the hospital. The eight-year-old is an epileptic. After three months the baby is still listless, though the three-year-old has picked up some and will occasionally return a smile or reach out for something. All the children are behind in school, although two seem unusually bright.

These are the little lambs of God that the Restoration Corps broods over. "I don't know," says Dennis, "that we will matter in their lives, but they have come to matter in ours. They have changed us."

One night the mother called at midnight, as she often did, to report to Muriel that she and four of the children had been baptized. "We can't make it by ourselves," she said. "I know we need God."

"I knew it also," said Muriel. "Since going through what we have with this family, I know they need more than a house, or us, or money. All these things I have, and more, but in themselves they are not enough."

5

The Frontier Church
and Psychiatry

The church of tomorrow which moves with power and proclaims with any authority the Kingdom of God will have to be familiar with the findings of depth psychology and use these findings to minister not only to the wounded and broken of the world, but to its own people. This is part of what it will mean to be a church on an inward journey—a church concerned with the wholeness of man. It is a difficult concept to accept, for it stirs unfamiliar and uneasy feelings in us. It strikes at our idealization of the Christian as the whole person and the Christian community as the "saved" community. Even churches which have incorporated pastoral counseling programs into their ministry do not see those programs in terms of the whole congregation, but in terms of the sick, and the sick as those set apart.

We can no longer do this in the Church of the Saviour. The therapy program involves too many of us. In its first two years, over 150 in our congregation of 250 have participated. Of those 150 persons, 70 were in the group therapy program from three months to two years. And still the program goes on, with six groups made up of between 6 and 8 persons each. These groups meet once a week and are open-ended, which means that there are persons leaving them and coming into them all the time. In addition, over 10 per cent of our congregation has been in depth analysis with psychiatrists outside our community life, whose religious backgrounds we do not know. Even with this experience, there are many of us who still survey the whole field of psychiatry with mixed feelings, which include often a need to find the therapeutic program related to faith and the spiritual pilgrimage. For this reason, I paused before writing the above figures. I wondered if they would startle our friends who find hope and strength in the church here, for surely they will stir in others some of the same questions they have stirred in us. Yet for this reason I include them. I am neither theologian nor psychiatrist and I cannot add to the literature that has been written on the subject of religion and psychiatry. I can write only as a member of a congregation who can speak experientially of what is often only written of in the abstract.

Most of us have not moved in the sophisticated and psychiatrically oriented circles one finds in large cities. If in the past we have gone to psychiatrists for help, we went, like Nicodemus, by night. This is to say that our best friends did not guess. When it was possible, the fact was also hidden from our families. I am reminded of T. S. Eliot's lines:

> And now you live dispersed on ribbon roads,
> And no man knows or cares who is his neighbour
> Unless his neighbour makes too much disturbance.*

In the Church of the Saviour we live in community, and you cannot live in community and hide your problems. In fact, community will bring into light problems which, though they are yours, are often hidden even from you. Relationships in depth will always

---

* T. S. Eliot, *Choruses from "The Rock,"* Collected Poems 1909-1962 (New York, Harcourt, Brace & World, Inc., 1930), p. 188. Used by permission of Harcourt, Brace & World, Inc., and of Faber and Faber Limited, London.

do that. Christian community probably comes the closest of any community to the family of our childhood, and all the unassimilated hurts and unresolved problems of that family come to light again in the context of the new "family of faith." Sometimes apparently well-adjusted persons come into the life of the church, people of action, ready to get on with the mission of the church, and then a few months or a year later things do not appear to be as well with them. They are actually much better off, because a lot of their activity had been motivated by anxiety of one kind or another, or simply the need to belong. Others are afraid of relationships in depth and discover that, while they yearn for community, they back away when people get too close. Still others find stirring in them yearnings that had been quieted and are now raised to life by the life around. The reasons are different for each person, but the experience is always pain. No real growth takes place without pain. Nothing is born into the consciousness without suffering.

Some ask us if the commitment of the Church of the Saviour is due to the fact that its people have more need than other congregations. We have reflected on that question and we answer No, though it probably can be said that we have more consciousness of need than is found in most places. But then, is not this essential for the hearing of the Gospel? Christ makes clear to whom he is speaking when he says, "It is not the healthy that need a doctor, but the sick. Go and learn what that text means, 'I require mercy, not sacrifice.' I did not come to invite virtuous people, but sinners."

Also, those working in the field of mental health are giving serious consideration to theories that maintain that personality growth does not take place without periods of disintegration. When it seems to ourselves and to others that we are flying to pieces inside, it may be in order to integrate at a higher level of personality. This theory seems borne out by adolescence, which, though a period of turmoil and upheaval, is also a period of marked growth. In their own way, middle age and old age do not permit us to travel on the same plateau; they bring their own psychological upheaval—the breaking up of the old in order to embrace the new.

The fear of age in our society is based on the loss of the spiritual dimension of life, so that we miss God's design written into the fabric of our lives, and do not see that each period of life calls us to a new level of being. The temptation is to resist. The old land is familiar. We have built over the years the house we live in. Even if we do not like it, it seems safer than the unknown. But God would show us a new land and have us live in a new house, and He churns up the old land and lets the winds beat and floods come. If we are wise and will wake from our sleep, we will leave the old and build a new dwelling in the land that He will show to those who ask. All the other crises of life that make for upheaval in our emotions have the same creative potential for growth and deeper understanding, but the potential for disaster also exists. It is possible to drown in the undertow if the proper support is not there, and this is where the community must sometimes draw upon the resources of psychiatry.

We may need most to pity the man who has had no problems too big for him. He has no remembrance of pain and loss and a crying in the night which will let him hear this in the life of another. Perhaps of men he is the most lost—lost to himself and to a world acquainted with grief.

One thing we can know about the neighborhood where we live: in addition to the special times of crisis and stress that come to us, there is deep trouble in the lives of its people. You cannot have one out of three marriages failing, one out of every five hospital beds occupied by a mental patient, and five million alcoholics without having a stricken country. Add to this juvenile delinquency, crime, dope addiction, gambling, retarded children and illegitimate children, and then contemplate for a moment the havoc wrought in the emotional life of those who are closely bound up with one alcoholic. It is easier then to grasp that these figures do not stand by themselves, but fan out to include millions of others in their net. Remember also that they deal only with some of the grave emotional sicknesses of our land—the neighbor who "makes too much disturbance." What of jealousy and envy and aggression, which plague us all and make desperately difficult the relationships that have been given us as gifts? Boredom, apathy, meaninglessness, also have high places on the modern world's list of anxieties

And yet, somehow, we keep our lives so well hidden from one another that we do not guess that we are not alone. Distrust is among our subtle illnesses. We were given hearts for "reciprocal trust," but fear has built high walls, and even that must not be guessed. We are afraid of being hurt, and when we talk we make ourselves vulnerable. What we say can be used against us or betray our loyalty to another, and so we add isolation to our own burden and the burden of others.

One of our members spent two years in another congregation, was active in the life of the church and a member of one of its prayer groups. In the week before she left that community to return here, friends came to visit and for the first time talked of their problems and made confession. She was moving out of the area, and at last there was someone with whom their secrets were safe.

Those of our people who are free enough to talk about their participation in therapy programs with friends outside our life find that the biggest shock to others is that someone "normal" is doing this. One of our members who occasionally speaks at other churches always talks about her experience in the therapy program here. "That is a lot more real," she says, "than talking about church programing. Afterward the people who come up to me are free to say what they think and feel and what bothers them, because I am free to talk about what I struggle with. We have something to say to each other." Trust has called forth trust. The first time the courage came to her was at a coffee klatch of women in the neighborhood. The talk was the light exchange that always characterized these gatherings. When it turned to psychiatry, a lot of glib banter was introduced and the jesting comment—"maybe I should get on the couch." Into that conversation was dropped the information that she was in therapy. "I couldn't have done it," she said, "if I hadn't been feeling angry at their smugness—everything seemed so right with them." Their assurance that she didn't seem a bit unusual was poor comfort, and she left feeling that she had risked her life in the neighborhood. The next day, however, two of the women came to call and another telephoned. They wanted to talk about themselves and the possibility of therapy being helpful to them.

We think we live in a sophisticated age that is over the shock of Freud and accepts modern psychiatry. This impression is reinforced by college courses and articles in popular journals which give us a reading knowledge of the subject, but as a science it is still suspect—even by the medical profession which often seems the most threatened. The psychosomatic origin of many diseases has been well established, but we cannot afford to acknowledge the relationship between mind and body for fear the stigma attached to psychiatric visits would then attach to visits to the family physician. The safest thing is to think of psychiatry in terms of the disturbed, and not in terms of ourselves or our "normal" neighbors. If we can write therapy off for others, then we can write it off for ourselves, which means we will not have to encounter the frightening unknown of our own inner world.

Even though our awareness may be dim, we have enough intimation of something moving beneath the surface of our lives to want to leave it alone. We are afraid of the untested strength of our own feelings. We will ask ourselves no questions, or if we do, they will be the wrong ones. This will keep our precarious peace. No disturbing ideas will emerge. We will not think, and that will give us more time to act. We will be in step with the century of tranquilizers, and no one will say that we do not have health. We will so protect ourselves against disruptive influences that we will not even know that we dwell behind walls. We will not ask the question, "Who am I?" or wonder where we come from or where we go. We will not hear the call of God in Christ, which is always a call to embrace life—a call to freedom—a call to wholeness.

It is at the point of this call that the believer sometimes finds himself in conflict with his understanding of Christianity, for the promise is that Christ heals and that we will be whole if we cling to Him and to Him only. This has never ruled out the physician as a channel of God's healing power, but not so with the psychiatrist. There is still an intangible line drawn in our churches which makes the psychiatrist an intruder in the province of God, usurper of powers that belong to the divine. Within our own psychiatrically oriented church there are still people who say that if you are a Christian, you don't need an analyst. God will heal. He will show you all you need to know. This is, of course, true, but the assumption is that he would not choose an analyst as an agent of reconciliation. When it comes to the troubled heart, the feeling often is that God must heal directly. It must happen as we pray, or read scripture, or worship. This is what the legend says, and it is deep in our feelings. We say it in a hundred ways. We struggle through a maze of doubts and give psychiatry no place in the Christian pilgrimage. This can become especially bewildering to those who go to analysts and experience healing. The feeling is apt to be that psychiatry succeeded where Christianity failed. "After all, I was faithful and asked Christ to help and no help came. I asked the analyst for help and he gave it. He is the one who saves . . . the one who heals."

The problem of relating faith and psychiatry appears at another place. The Christian says, "I believe in psychiatry, but I would not want to go to anyone who is not Christian." The reason given is that one is not whole unless the spiritual dimension of his life is included in the analysis. But this does not explain why we would not also demand of our doctors and teachers that they deal with us on a spiritual level. Do we ask it of the psychiatrist because deep in us we know he works with matters of the soul, that he is a guide on the journey inward that Christianity calls us to take? Do we know intuitively that psychiatry is concerned with the coming of the Kingdom within?

But then, surely, of all people the Christian will not need his therapist to be a Christian. He can claim the resources of the Church to help him complete his inward journey and to give him hints of the land in which he finds himself. If anyone needs an analyst whose life is rooted in something beyond himself, it is the unchurched, for it is the unbeliever who is most apt to be without an interpreter. It is he who is apt to make a religion of psychiatry and to want to win converts to the way. It is he who still must find meaning and a name for the city toward which he journeys.

But perhaps it is not only this that makes the Christian ask for a Christian therapist. Perhaps he is afraid that his faith has shallow roots, and that the doubts in his heart will be changed into questions, and the questions receive answers, and the answers shake the ground on which he stands. Are we not most threatened by that which has most potential to destroy our security? Is not

Paul the classical example of this? He struggled not to hear the voice speaking within, which could change the whole order of his life, making him an outcast among his own people, jobless and alone. What was the slaughter of the Christians but angry defense against the force of truth that was closing in on him and sweeping before it the dogma around which his life was integrated?

Some of our fears we can put aside. The psychiatrist—Jew or Gentile—is not out to make us over in his image. He has no beliefs or goals to impose. If he is a real guide, he is committed to helping each person find the truth of his own life. "Work out your own salvation with fear and trembling." He is the reconciler who would help us be aware of the conflicts within that make for conflicts without. He is the man of faith, for he believes in the healing forces of our own psyches. Dr. Carl G. Jung said of analysts, "We have to do with men and women whose way of life is so individual that no counselor, however wise, could prescribe the way that is uniquely right for them. Therefore we have to teach them to listen to their own natures, so that they can understand from within themselves what is happening."*

Those wonderful new prophets in Christendom who call the Church to structure her life for mission to the world, and plead with us to hear God speaking through the world, are often closed to the possibility that God may be speaking to us through the still struggling movement of psychoanalysis. The church reformers know with certainty that the church must strip for action, and they often look askance at any deep involvement with self, which means to them disengagement with the world. What is lost sight of is that the disengagement has already taken place, and that the purpose of counseling in the minister's study or psychiatrist's office is to help a person discover his real self. To the extent that we are lost to ourselves, to that extent we are lost to the world. Conversely, the man who finds himself, finds his world.

But—the argument will run—can we not be ministers to one another, can we not be the listening person? And the answer is a thousand times Yes. This is what we are called to be. The home is to be the first listening center for the child, which will equip him

* C. J. Jung, *The Development of Personality, Collected Works,* Vol. 17 (New York: Pantheon Books, 1954), p. 62.

for his own listening ministry, but this so often does not happen, and the Christian home is no exception. Freud's limited view of Christianity evolved out of his work with patients raised in Christian homes. Every day we are in touch with people raised in the church who have not known one person in their lives who gave them opportunity to speak out of the depths of their being. One young woman summed it up in these words, "My friends told me that I did not need a psychiatrist, that all I needed was a good friend to listen. The only thing was that I didn't have one friend who could listen for five minutes at the point of my experience and not her own, let alone fifty minutes. At first I was literally paying the psychiatrist just to listen." Certainly there are listeners in the world, but their number is small. "The harvest truly is plenteous, and the laborers few." We know ourselves how poorly we listen, but the reason is that we have not listened to ourselves, and he who has not heard himself speak does not hear another.

What the church come of age will know is that psychiatry in all its forms can be used to equip her for mission, but more than this, psychiatry can be the church on mission. The church which takes the shape of psychiatric clinics and halfway houses and counseling centers and mental health programs will be the church with its spires raised in an age which is fast being born. This means that churches must be in conversation with their young people choosing a career and help them be aware of the need for psychiatrists, therapists, social workers, and nurses, not only as a vocation in the world but a vocation of the church in the world. Right now in "enlightened" America there is only one psychiatrist for every thirteen thousand people. There is something incredible about that figure, but it reflects an age which, while rocketing into outer space, does not pause to ask what we will do when we set foot on some foreign planet. The task is simply to get there. It will matter very little whether we arrive or not, if the peoples of the world are not on an inward journey. A new age demands a new age of the spirit, which will not come, apart from a deeper understanding of self.

One of the Hasidic sayings reads, "God said to Abraham: 'Get thee out of thy country, and from thy kindred, and from thy father's house, unto the land that I will show thee,' God says to man: 'First, get you out of your country, that means the dimness you have inflicted on yourself. Then out of your birthplace, that means out of the dimness your mother inflicted on you. After that, out of the house of your father, that means out of the dimness your father inflicted on you. Only then will you be able to go to the land that I will show you.' "*

* Martin Buber, *Ten Rungs: Hasidic Sayings* (New York: Shocken Books, 1947), p. 70.

6

The Potter's House

Week after week a man came alone to The Potter's House, ordered espresso coffee, sipped it silently, and left. Then one night he asked his waitress the question that strangers most often ask: "Who runs this place?" There is usually some awareness that this information is not ordinarily demanded in eating places, and sometimes an explanation is given. He said that many times in the year past he had dropped in on his way home from work. "I have seen new enterprises start before," he said, "and there is always great enthusiasm. Everything shines, and then the sheen begins to wear away. You see the edges being cut and pretty soon the frayed look comes. After that it's not long before there is just another eating place. This hasn't happened here and there must be a reason."

This conversation took place in the first year of The Potter's House. I remember it, not because I was his waitress and carefully chose my words to tell him that it was run by a church and staffed by members of the congregation, but because his ready response was, "Ah . . . commitment is the answer." He used the word that I hesitated to use, and let me know that he had stumbled on the

secret. He had grasped what those of us in the church are sometimes slow to understand, the understanding of which is essential
for the church on mission.

The Potter's House is now seven years old, and the sheen is still
there. The burlap tablecloths have faded to more muted tones, and
chipped cups do appear on the tables, but the spindly-legged chairs
that were collapsing have been replaced by more solid ones, and
underfoot is a thick new carpet that appears like old flooring and
adds to the rustic but elegant look of wood walls and candlelight
and Danish lamps. There have been packed nights and times when
the room has vibrated to the spontaneous singing of the freedom
songs, and yet it always seems possible to stand in its peace.

One man who had put to himself a question concerning The
Potter's House gave his answer to the cashier. He said, "I have
mulled over the reason of this place and I think I understand. You
can't give beauty to the world, but you can give it to that little
place where you are."

It seems to us also that The Potter's House with its soft browns
and dim lights and hand stonework is its own excuse for being. But
this may be prejudice, for if the world often asks, "Who runs this
place?" the Church, which knows the answer to that question,
most often asks, "Why?" "How does the church make its witness
in a coffee house?" John Perry raised the question for us all in an
article entitled "Coffee Houses: Evangelism or Evasion?"*

The question is well asked, for the witness of a coffee house is
not always clear even for those involved. It is possible for it to be
evangelism for some and evasion for others. With over 950 church-
sponsored coffee houses now in existence and many more in the
planning stage, we need to reflect on the essential elements of this
form of mission, and to share our thoughts with one another. We
have to do this from time to time in our own coffee house, which
requires seventy persons to staff it each week. Each of the seventy
is committed to being there one night a week. We meet on our
chosen nights an hour before The Potter's House opens at 8:00
P.M. and seldom get away until an hour after the midnight closing.
This totals six hours for each person and 420 man hours in every
week.

* *motive magazine*, March 1965.

Most of these hours are put in after a day's work, so that someone is always asking the question, "Is it worth it? If this is just another coffee house, then let those whose business it is to run coffee houses run this one." In the first years it cost, in addition to all the volunteer working hours, $3,000 a year, which was added reason to question its purpose. It was not enough for most of us to feel a rightness about the coffee-house ministry. If we did not need to define it for ourselves, we needed to do it for others. The definition was finally summarized in three words, "presence, service, dialogue."

The word *presence* appearing now and then in the literature of the Church and in the conversation between churches, was seized on as descriptive of the ministry of the coffee house. For us it gave a name to that which had no name, and yet we were constantly asked to interpret what had not been interpreted for us, "What do you mean by presence?" Could we simply say that through us the church was present in the coffee house? Did this word, "presence" mean our presence, or did it speak of another Presence? "Wherever two or three are gathered in my name, there I am." Was it possible that these familiar words were true words? Now that we were asked to act as though they were, a blasphemous doubt was out in the open. It is one thing to cling to a mystical belief in your private heart and another to hold it out in the market place. Could we be so presumptuous as to claim that because we were there, a Presence was there? Was the question, "Who runs this place?" witness to that Presence? One confirming word was written on a fifty-dollar check left as a tip on a busy Saturday night. In the lower left hand after the printed word "For:_____" was written "Inspiration."

Then there was the young couple who conducted their courtship in the coffee house, seemingly oblivious of their surroundings. When they married and moved away, what they missed most was The Potter's House. "There came over us the strange feeling that there was something different at the coffee house. We vowed if ever we got back to Washington, we would ask for an explanation." We have this story because they jubilantly returned to ask their questions, and in asking them bore witness to the church of the ministry of presence.

The ministry of presence came as astounding news to many of us who staff The Potter's House, which is in itself revealing. While its sophisticated atmosphere kept us from entertaining the thought of any old-time evangelism, we nonetheless secretly felt that the effectiveness of the coffee-house mission was somehow dependent upon someone's saying the wise thing at the appropriate moment. It had never occurred to us with any force that we could just relax and *"be."* We had given lip service to the doctrine that God is the evangelist and that the Spirit is at work in the coffee house, but the fact is that most of us never really believed it until the world came back again and again to bear witness to that Spirit. This, in itself, was an unexpected turn in the order of things.

Service, in its own way, was as difficult a concept to grasp as presence, though intellectually it was easier. The fact that our very presence made a difference seemed to us, when we were preoccupied with self, a boastful claim. We were much more ready to embrace service as a form of witness. It better suited our image of humbleness. Christ had taken the form of a servant, and we would. When He could have issued orders, He took a basin and washed the feet of His friends. It was unquestionably clear that the church needed to recover its servant role. As for the activists among us, the emphasis on doing rather than being just generally made more sense, and therefore seemed the more intelligent approach. In the end it proved easy for no one. There was no saint among us who ever made any effort to be first by being last.

In the first place, we discovered that we were all quite individual in our approach to work. We simply did not agree on what constituted work. There were always the industrious and energetic who, not being content with their own labors, felt it important that all be equally conscientious. They harbored feelings of being imposed upon, and with good reason, since they could never walk around the undone tasks with the apparent ease of others. Then there were among us those warmhearted, gregarious people who had only seen service as a means to an end. When asked to join a table, they fell easily into long conversations with the guests and held discourse on a great variety of subjects. It usually did not occur to them to wonder what was happening to the guests at their other tables. The witness of service was completely lost to consciousness in the witness of dialogue. They assumed that others would take up their responsibilities, or that the necessity of offending a few coffeehouse guests was unimportant, since the temporary suspension of table service furthered the real mission of the coffee house. We also had in our company those who were simply lazy and always managed to evade working. In a way they were easier to cope with than the brethren who did very little but were completely unaware of how little, and came to the end of an evening genuinely exhausted from their efforts. Broad as these categories are, they hardly describe us all, and certainly not those who quietly and efficiently went about their servant tasks, letting the rest of us scream at one another. We who had wanted to be in the market place so that the world might observe "how they love one another," found ourselves giving thanks that the world was not always looking.

In our servant role we were up against the large question of authority that faces the mission church. We found that, not only did we not want authority with its special responsibilities, but neither did we want to risk delegating it to others. That another person could tap us on the shoulder and say, "Clear that table," outraged something deep in us. We discovered that the servant bit was all right provided we were doing what it pleased us to do, and doing it on our own terms—and also, provided it was generally known that we were not servants but simply assuming the role. Gordon Cosby tells the story of a time he was at one of the large universities, where he delivered three addresses. For the days that he was there, everyone called him Doctor. He corrected this several times, and they acknowledged his words but kept right on calling him Dr. Cosby. He didn't press the point, since it began to seem as though the prestige of the academic community might make it important for their speaker to have a title. After several days of this, he arrived back in Washington in time to serve and "bus" tables at The Potter's House. It was a particularly crowded night, and there had been no opportunity to be with several tables that were waiting for him to join them for conversation on church renewal. He was hurrying to clear a table when a customer snapped his fingers and said in a surly tone, "Hey, boy!" "There arose in me," said Gordon, "the feeling, 'Don't you know who I am? I don't have to do this.'"

If we learned that the servant heart is not naturally given to us, this did not mean that the witness of service was not made in spite of us. It is best illustrated by the concerned question of a young woman. She stopped her waitress and said, "Do you see that man over there waiting on tables? I was once his secretary. He was a promising young lawyer then. I want to know what happened to him that he is waiting on tables?" Her waitress told her as best she could what had happened to him.

Those who frequented the coffee house on any regular basis noted that the staff was different every night. What seemed most impressive to them was that these people volunteered their time week after week. Many assumed that money was the motivating factor, which gave rise to another question, "What does the church do with the money it makes?" We explained that, popular as the coffee house was, it was only open four hours a night for six days a week, and that it was difficult to cover expenses while operating only twenty-four hours a week. "Then, why do it?" is the question that always follows this statement. Mahlon Carrington, whose approach is uncomplicated, says, "When they ask me this, I say, 'You're having a good time, aren't you?' They say 'Yes,' and then I say, 'Well, it's worthwhile, then.' Others take the opportunity to say something about the ferment that is going on in the churches and the quest for forms that will make the church relevant and enable it not only to address the world, but be addressed by it. The task in this kind of conversation is to acquaint those who have not been to church in years with the new church that is coming of age. The labor that was poured into the decor and the changing art exhibits was another type of service which bore witness to the changing church and led us into all kinds of conversation. The lighting system was what impressed one man, "I can't believe it," he said. "I just can't believe that any church would have a lighting engineer that good."

Dialogue, under which heading we put proclaiming the faith, was seldom unrelated to service or presence. Dialogue flowed easily out of service, or came in the moment of being present to another. It was even related to silence. We began to know the unimportance of words and to understand "the firmament proclaims" and "day to day pours forth speech." This happened at The Potter's House, not unlike the way it had happened to Jeremiah, who, watching a potter at his work, heard God's voice and God's words. The difference was that it seemed, from our perspective, less dramatic and always to take a long time. There are few burning bushes and many a long desert stretch.

There was the angry woman who came in the very early days of The Potter's House and told us that, a few months before, her good job had come to an end. As, week after week, she trudged the streets looking for another job, she became more frightened and more angry. We spent hundreds of hours talking to her and contacting people who might be helpful to her. Every poor lead she followed added to her anger until it seemed to us that she would talk herself out of any possibility of employment. Then one day she was offered a job which six months before she would not have taken, but which now seemed right to her. She had treated us like enemies, but now that she was able to feel some security about the future, this changed. Though she never moved into the life of the church, and remained a silent, serious figure in the coffee house, there was no one on the staff with whom she did not exchange a greeting. Even with the conversation between us kept at a bare minimum, she was still familiar with what was happening in the various missions, and from time to time wrote a check for one, which she always pushed briskly into an appropriate hand when she was leaving.

Though it often happened that the dialogue at the coffee house took place in silence, this is not because we did not have a love for words and a belief in the power of the Word, but because we knew that there were not many words that could be a "deep pool, a flowing stream, a fountain of life." Most of us were unchurched, or had come back into the church after being away from it for years. We knew God as a listening God who had waited a long time to be in conversation with us. We also had experienced in the group therapy program of the church what it was to be listened to on the human level and to be able to question and to search. Though sometimes dogmatism crept in and it was said of a person, "He is not Christian," or of a statement, "that is not Christian," the atmosphere was usually one of openness—a willingness for others to come to their own conclusions. We have learned to trust another to find his own way in his own time.

A few of us had been deeply influenced by the writings of Martin Buber. On the back cover of our menu we had stated: "The Potter's House is to provide a place of meeting between persons," aware of the depth and height that Buber had given to this word "meeting." His writings confirmed what experience had proved, that meeting does not depend upon agreement, but can take place in attack or the clash of differing viewpoints. We did not often know how much change came in others, but we were sometimes aware that a change came in us. Maurice Friedman, speaking at Pendle Hill on Martin Buber, had said, "The 'Where art thou,' to Adam, is addressed to every man." "Where art thou in your life?" This is the question the dialogue of The Potter's House most often raised in our own lives, and it would seem natural to assume that it was also raised for others. Sometimes a person would come back three or five years later to finish a conversation. One such person was a young artist whose abstract paintings hung on our walls for six weeks. Every review of his work gave indication that he was on the way up, and this was also his own answer to the "Where art thou?" When his show was over his visits to The Potter's House stopped. He didn't return until five years later, when his answer to the "Where art thou?" was "I am dying. I am a man dying inside."

As the first year of The Potter's House moved into the second, we began to know at another level that the ministry of presence and service and dialogue was bound up with our own life of worship. The fact is that we are not people who are naturally present to another or present to the moment. It is too easy to be caught up in all the stimuli of our surroundings, to lose ourselves in outward events. Or, at another extreme, to be lost in inner events or the world of fantasy. This condition is often described as being "a million miles away," or expressed in the words, "He isn't with it," or the order, "Get with it!" We are going through the motions, but we are the absentee landlords of our persons. Because we are absent to ourselves, we are absent to others and the task at hand.

We are not present as the Church in the world because we are not present to the indwelling Lord of the Church. We cannot call another into that Presence because we ourselves have lost awareness of it. We are running down a million avenues, instead of standing in the moment with the moment God.

Long before the first year had passed, we learned that we tended to avoid putting on the servant role in its entirety when it threatened our prestige or our ease or convenience. Could we extend our gracious servant hospitality beyond the coffee-house walls if our patrons happened to tell us what their real needs were and how we actually could be of service? Would we draw back then? "Friend, what we had in mind was a cup of coffee. The limits of our service are defined by the number of items on the menu, and we are even out of some of these." Even if we were enabled to bear another's burden, could we let that other bear ours and so meet him as a brother? In whose service are we? Do we serve only our own human need to serve, or could we also move into the service of Truth—into the service of Him who is Truth?

And what of the life of dialogue? Did our words bear witness to our own confusion, or did they point beyond ourselves to the God and Father of our Lord Jesus Christ? Did Jesus come bearing witness to the fact that all things go well for Christians? Or rather, that there can be dialogue between heaven and earth? "Into thy hands I commit my spirit," bears witness to a God who makes reply. Was there in our own lives that dialogue to say that beyond the world's despair there is One who hears our agonizing question, "Why hast Thou forsaken me?"

The witness of presence, service, and dialogue when defined and pondered helped us renew our commitment to the disciplines of prayer and devotion on which The Potter's House was founded. It became clear that it is one thing to join a group and serve coffee, and another to be saved from the narrow limits of our ordinary responses.

The coffee house had been intended as our ministry to the "up and out," but it proved to be many-faceted. If we confronted the world, we also confronted ourselves. We who talked so much about accepting the unacceptable couldn't get along with a little group of people who came every night and offended our sense of decorum by pushing tables together and bringing their own birthday cakes. We discovered how defensive we could be, not only in the face of hostility, but of the well-meant critical word. We learned that piety can cloak aggression and that forgiveness is not only costly to God, but to anyone who forgives, and costly, also, to him who does not forgive. The lessons came in a hundred ways. Grace came in those moments when God broke through and the conflicting elements within were united and we were not legion but one.

The church today which is concentrating on mission and raising the theological issues for a technological age tends to discount institutional forms. One catches the feeling that all the churches need to do is release their thousands of members so that they can be the church-in-the-world. Very little is said about what will happen after the theological issue is raised and the Word proclaimed. In one way the new missionary strategy is not far removed from a mass religious meeting: there is nowhere to go when it is over. There is no visible community to be a part of. One has heard a word, but it may be the last. There is little recognition that we each hear God speak only what we are ready to hear. Openness to the holy comes at different depths of being. Max Warren stresses that the church has more than to penetrate the world and witness to the world the purpose of God. "The Church," he writes, "is not only an army on the march . . . . The Church is also a hospital for those being healed from sin, a community in which men and women grow to be saints . . . the time is overdue when writers about the Church's mission in the world cease to talk as if the Church can, *qua* institution, discharge its total missionary task."*

The community of The Potter's House includes the poor, and this has been for the healing of us all. The jobs of coffee-maker and dishwasher and cleaning help are the three paid positions. A teen-ager from Junior Village was employed for the first time in his life by The Potter's House. He had grown up in Junior Village, an institution for homeless children. He had never had a job, and certainly no home in the city, but he had reached the age of eighteen when it was required that he leave Junior Village. In a time of bewildering and anxious transition, The Potter's House

* *Ecumenical Review*, Vol. XVII, No. 3, p. 222.

was for him a supporting community. When he went into the army and got his first leave, it was The Potter's House he called to announce, "I'm coming home!" Other teen-agers came after him. In more recent years we have hired to do these jobs friends we came to know through our work in the slums of Washington. They have widened our small world. I remember the hours that Esther Dorsey spent getting the fourteen-year-old daughter of Lucille admitted to a home for unwed mothers. She told Lucille that the girl would be taken care of and that an agency would place her baby in a good home. Esther was feeling an immense relief and, as Lucille was already raising two grandchildren together with her own fatherless brood, she expected her to share this relief. Instead a look of amazed horror came over Lucille's face. "Esther," she finally said, "this is my own grandchild, my own flesh and bone. We don't do that kind of thing in my family."

Perhaps it was Clarence who gave us our most dramatic encounter with a world outside our own. He had a long record of housebreaking and burglary in Washington when he came to work at The Potter's House. He fitted easily into the life of the coffee house. He was not only an efficient worker, but he had a gentle spirit and sensitivity to need. Clarence was also a gentleman. No woman ever lifted a heavy package while he was around or walked unescorted to her car. We became acquainted with Clarence's past after we found him stretched out in front of the open safe, the combination in his hand, peacefully sleeping off a night of barhopping.

While we pressed no charges, this did not keep Clarence out of prison. His activities were too widespread. A letter to Esther two years later read:

DEAR ESTHER,
It has taken me quite some time and nerve to write this letter and even now I am apprehensive about it. After reading my return address, you should be aware that I am in prison. My crime this time is a violation of the narcotic law (possession and sale). It seems that I have gone from bad to worse and perhaps this revelation will cause you to tear this letter to shreds, but I hope not. I can't give any plausible reason for

my present predicament nor will I offer any excuses. I can only say that the lure of the easy (? ? ?) dollar was too strong for me. What motivated me to write you is a question I can't answer and if someone should ask me, I doubt if I could tell him. Having an abundance of leisure time on my hands could be a reason, anyway it started me to thinking and my thoughts centered around The Potter's House and everyone associated with it. My thinking also made me realize that I spent some very happy and unforgettable times there; and it was one of the very few times that I was really and truly happy. If I should be fortunate enough to travel around the country, I doubt very seriously if I would find a more wonderful group of people than there is at The Potter's House. Even after they knew about my past criminal activities, they still accepted and sincerely liked me for myself and this has rarely happened in my life. If I must single out anyone who treated me with warmth and understanding then the honor must go to you and the Rev. Gordon Cosby. This doesn't take anything from the others because they were swell to me also and I like them very much, but where you two are concerned, I guess I am sort of prejudiced. I felt very strongly about you and the others, but the business with the safe was a funny way of showing my appreciation for acceptance. My psychiatrist here tells me that I am afraid to let people get close to me and when they begin to I find some way to hurt them. I don't know about this and maybe he is right, but I do know that I have never been more ashamed and sorry about anything than I am about that safe incident—I would like to send greetings to each person, but I can't remember them all, but to those I do I send my love and best wishes. . . . Bye for now and with this letter comes what you and the others will always have—my gratitude for knowing all of you and my fondest thoughts.

Ever yours,
CLARENCE

Clarence's mother had had five husbands and eighteen children, which is a plausible reason for his present predicament.

There are many who feel that the only way to help the poor is to live with them in their slum neighborhoods, but obviously everyone cannot make this kind of response. Our experiences at The Potter's House let us know that there are other ways and that the medium of work is one. We have Christians with their own businesses who could make those businesses work communities. Their books may not show the same profits at the end of the year, but only because earnings used to further the Kingdom of God are recorded in other ledgers.

The Potter's House gave us our first corporate entree into the world of business. Esther became a member of the Business Men's Association and was first elected their secretary and then their delegate to the Community Council.

The ministry of The Potter's House remains threefold: to those of us who work there, the world, and the Church. Increasingly it becomes a place of exchange for the Church all over the world which is groping with the missionary structure of the local congregation in our time. Often it has been a place of painful confrontation for us all. One night a tense young man flew through the door, pushed past the waiting line, and said breathlessly to the host, "I must speak to Gordon Cosby." The host said, "I am Gordon Cosby and if you can wait a few minutes, I can be with you." When a break came and Gordon was able to join him at a table, the young man, a minister, began, "I'm in trouble." Though this was a sentence that punctuated his story, his polite, anxious words did not make it easy to grasp his plight. He said that he had written to the Church of the Saviour stating that he would be visiting Washington with his youth group. He had requested lodging so that they could spend a few days with the frontier church at work in the inner city. His letter had been passed on to the social action group of his own denomination. They had found rooms for him in a Negro church in southeast Washington. "The kids are there now," he said. "You have to help me out. I'm really in trouble." "Could you say a little more about your trouble?" Gordon asked. "The church," he said, "is Negro. These kids are all white and their parents won't like it. They will hold me responsible. Isn't there some place at your church where they can stay?"

Gordon explained to him that we had no available rooms, but

that even if we did, we would not be able to help him offend his Negro hosts who were offering him hospitality. Gordon then outlined the two possibilities which were open to the young man. "You can," he said, "get in touch with your denomination headquarters who have a lot of resources and won't have any difficulty finding rooms, or you can stay where you are and use this as a teaching situation for your young people."

The Minister of Youth left uncomforted. The next day we heard that he and his group were lodged in a white suburban parsonage, from which they could safely observe the mission church in the inner city. But for every group that was ready only to observe, there were a hundred others that wanted to be involved and wrote to ask for the opportunity. We had no plan, but part of the conversation with other churches at The Potter's House centered on the question of how to engage the young in mission.

The Potter's House had always been a place for dialogue between Roman Catholics and Protestants. But in the spring of 1967 what we had sometimes theorized about became an actuality. We were acquainted with a group of young seminarians at the Theological College of the Catholic University of America in Washington, D.C., and when The Potter's House Sunday night group lost half its members to a new mission, we invited them to join the group. The young men responded enthusiastically. To be in the same mission—or "apostolate," as they called it—bound by the same covenant, seemed to us all another step in our dialogue.

Gordon wrote a letter to the university inviting the students to participate, and permission was granted. We had expected to excuse our new mission members early so that they could be at the college at the required hour of 11:00 P.M. but the Rector told the students, "No, we want you to participate fully in this mission." He was a man whose life was invested in old forms, who was saying Yes to the new. This spirit and trust on the part of those responsible for the guidance of these young seminarians seemed like a Word for our churches in this uncertain age. In our own congregation we have sometimes wondered if the denominational structures of Protestantism were reformable, but then there is an occasion like this when the new happens in our midst, and the promise of change comes up like a star above our own individual lives and our corporate life. For the first time the Sunday night Potter's House mission named co-moderators—Marty McDaniel, interning with us from the Presbyterian Church, U.S. and Joe Miller, preparing for the Roman Catholic priesthood.

Other Potter's House groups were working with different kinds of projects, including a coffee house in a slum area. The Potter's House is seven years old, and maybe this is the reason one can discern the outlines of something called "change." Seven has about it the sound of completeness—the rounding off of the old, the possibility of the new.

7

New and Old Forms
of Worship

THE COFFEE HOUSE CHURCH*

We had talked casually at times about having Sunday worship services at The Potter's House, but always there were some to say that the coffee-house crowd would claim that The Potter's House had been, after all, a gimmick to get people to church. If our own blue chapel at headquarters building had not ceased to hold us, the Coffee House Church probably never would have happened. As it was, we were crowded into halls at both services and obviously destined for the street. Our mission theology made it inconceivable that a church building program should ever be admitted into consciousness, let alone mentioned aloud. When an experimental church at The Potter's House was proposed once again, our grim

* This section on the Coffee House Church appeared in the March, 1966, issue of *Union Seminary Quarterly Review*, pp. 321-324.

sidewalk future gave us an openness we did not have earlier. When you are being thrust out, you consider what you ordinarily would not consider.

The proposal this time came from the group that staffed The Potter's House on Sunday night, which wanted to try the church services on an eight-weeks' trial basis. The church Council enthusiastically agreed. It seemed a *kairos* moment carrying an opportunity "imposed on us by God."

The traditional eleven o'clock hour was chosen because it fell between our two regular services at headquarters and made it impossible to be greedy and go to two services, which thought did occur. We let only our own congregation know about the new church. No announcement was ever made at The Potter's House. There we treated it like an underground church—not to be spoken of, unless one happened to identify oneself as Christian.

The laymen chosen to speak on the eight Sunday mornings were very different from each other. They were Abner Lall, scientist; Bud Wilkinson, potter; Bill Maloney, oceanographer; David Bourns, moderator of the Covenant Community; Alma and Bill Newitt, actress and chemist; David Mayer, of the State Department; Tom Hubers, insurance manager; and James Rouse, mortgage banker and developer. Each was told that the spoken presentation was to be restricted to fifteen minutes—twenty at the very longest.

That first Sunday, and thereafter, we arrived at nine in order to make two urns of coffee and arrange the tables so that six persons would be seated at each table and everyone would have the best possible view of the speaker. The worship bulletin, with a cover design by Lynn Trout, was put at each place and was in itself an invitation to worship. Hart Cowperthwait, who knows music and had installed our stereo tape recording system, checked each week with the speaker to make music an integral part of the service. It began at 10:45 and set the mood of worship, so that those coming in usually moved in silence to a table.

At 11:00 we began the reading of the coffee-house litany with the words, "Let us acknowledge and affirm that we gather as we live, in the Name of the Father, the Son, and the Holy Spirit." After the prayer of confession and absolution, the leader—everyone shied away from the word "preacher"—read the scripture and then gave his sermon. Again, we had to change the word "sermon" to "spoken meditation," since our lay leaders objected, and "sermon" also seemed out of place in a coffee house. Fifteen minutes of quiet came after the spoken meditation. The first few minutes were in complete silence, followed by faint strains of music, which slowly increased in volume. In the last five minutes of music we served coffee and rolls. Our "preacher" then received comments and questions from the floor. After lively and sometimes heated discussion, the formal worship was resumed with the words of commitment from the litany and closed with the benediction at 12:15. No one left, however, and it was always close to two o'clock before we could lock the doors.

Long before the series was over we knew that there had been initiated a form of worship that was significant for our own congregation and possibly the Church in our age. It was evident at many points. For one thing, the laity had responded with zest to the invitation to preach, which never would have happened if the setting had been a formal pulpit. We had volunteers say, "Call on me, if you get stuck," which was unheard of even in our unconventional experience of church. Our laymen from the beginning claimed the coffee house as their church. The second thing that became evident was that the Coffee House Church was not dependent upon brilliant preaching. The fact that the congregation had an opportunity to add to it, as well as to question it, made the presentation live. The authenticity of the message was also in the life of the person speaking, and over the weeks there was a cumulative effect. A different prophet each Sunday gave us to know that we were surrounded by a host of witnesses. Because no one personality dominated the Coffee House Church, and there was so little evidence of its being administered, it took on, in reflection, a numinous quality. A Presence became more and more real, and it became more and more believable who the Head of the Church was.

Another important factor was the breaking of bread that took place at the tables. After the first service someone suggested that we ought to give thanks before eating. The next Sunday we followed the suggestion and found that our words of blessing sounded "religious and artificial." The whole atmosphere was one of worship, which made words unnecessary. Many of us had the feeling that this was a Communion breakfast, and one person who passed the coffee and rolls found himself silently saying the words of the Lord's Table. So unmistakable were the symbols that we later spread a napkin over each plate of rolls.

Though sometimes the conversation was superficial or social, it was more often on an intense level. Introductions were waived, and people who had never been in conversation with one another were discussing such subjects as, "What do you mean by the Living God?" "How does one follow the narrow way?" "Is the disciplined devotional life necessary?" "What is life really about?" Sometimes the questions were given to us by the leader. More often they came out of the meditation or open exchange.

Above all was the experience of community. The gift of Christian community was often given and received. It was strange to look back on those mornings and know that you had discussed with strangers your own answer to God's "Where art thou?"

As the weeks went by the congregation grew. Friend told friend, and people who had not been to church for years ventured into the Coffee House Church. Some were intrigued by the setting and the opportunity to "answer back," as well as the absence of clergy. Occasionally, however, a professional did leave his congregation to be with us. Said one, "It's the best pulpit in town from the viewpoint that the preacher is not safe."

The new church gathering in a coffee house raises a sign for many. Those who are estranged from the church feel this might be different from the church they have left. Others have the feeling that anything as "way out" as worship in a coffee house is worth a try. The unstructured form makes special appeal to teen-agers and young adults. We are also freer to invite our friends. It is easier to talk about the coffee-house service to sophisticated suburbanites than about a conventional church service. We can invite a doctor to hear a doctor talk and an artist to hear an artist. In the early weeks before the proper notices had been tacked on the door, we even had a couple who were visiting Washington wander in for breakfast. Before they looked at the bulletin and discovered that the fare was not what they had in mind, the worship began. They were quickly caught up in the spirit of this new version of the storefront church, and went away several hours later expressing their appreciation, as well as shock, for just being there. We ourselves felt like a celebrating people given to proclaim that the Lord of the church is the Lord of the city. Sitting inside that storefront church, the figures moving on the street outside seemed forlorn and cheated of their invitation to the banquet.

Before the eight weeks' experimental church was over a new mission group had formed to carry on. The members listed as the marks of the new church:

1. The ministry of the laity
2. Dialogue within the context of worship
3. The experience of Christian community
4. Worship as mission

In the coffee house we had a vision, and in the vision the restaurants and factories and taverns of the city had become the worship halls of the church come of age.

THE OLD AND THE NEW

The coffee-house service was so appealing to some that at a meeting of our members we explored the possibility of changing our chapel at headquarters. It was suggested that we bring in tables and take the chairs out of traditional rows, transforming the room into a coffee-house setting. The possibility was simply raised to be sounded out in our hearts. No vote was to be taken or opinion recorded. With that threat removed, we had no outraged feelings to express and were free to give our immediate, though unconsidered, response.

The idea sparked flames, but did not catch fire anywhere. Even those who worshiped most often at the coffee house were glad to know that the traditional service was there to return to when the spirit moved. And then, we were reminded of those who had come to the coffee house and, missing the hymns and familiar litany, had said it was not for them. Also, even coffee-house enthusiasts had weeks when it seemed that everywhere they had been engaged in "meaningful" dialogue and exchange of insight and ideas. The need was for *meaningful* hearing—time to turn words in the quiet of the inner heart—to listen only to one's own questions and one's own response.

Reflecting on the vision of the Church at worship in supermarkets, theaters, and coffee houses, one can imagine a time in the future when it has not only come to pass but is commonplace. Cathedrals and steepled churches are only read about in books and produced in miniature for museums. The Church is at worship in skyscrapers, on roof gardens, and in factories. Onto this contemporary scene advances the "knight of faith"—the innovator—and he says to the assembled congregation sitting on desks and gazing out of windows that look on buildings and jet planes and sky highways, "Let us plan a place which is only intended for worship, and let us have an entirely new service where there is no conversation—only praise and confession and the word preached. Even the building," he exclaims excitedly, "shall point to God." Some will protest, but some will free him to build his cathedral, and there will be those who go to help.

In the next twenty years the church will move into an age when its structures will be in the places where life is being lived out, as well as "ground down." We can help to create these new forms, and at the same time wonder if they will give enough support to the man who cherishes an inner life.

Jesus said, ". . . every scribe who has been trained for the kingdom of heaven is like a householder who brings out of his treasure what is new and what is old" (Matt. 13:52, RSV). Surely it is mandatory to ask what kind of training allows us to do this, so that we can search it out. What makes us open to the past, so that even while scarred by it we can receive its treasure? Harvey Cox, speaking in our coffee house, said of the old Gospel songs that were part of his childhood, "I am getting so I can enjoy them." Gordon, speaking to some ministers about prayer and scripture, had one of them say to him, "You are talking to us about the roots out of which we come—the heritage we have lost."

And the future, what is it that can make us open, so that it is vibrant with possibilities rather than freighted with the threat of diminishing vitality? We can make even the future a flight from the past—the history of our life that we dare not examine. Perhaps we risk ourselves when we look to the past as well as when we look to the future. In our church we talk of the need to take risks, if we are to live our lives fully and follow that destiny which is unique for each soul. Sometimes we talk of this risk-taking as though it were something that one could just do, when it is very doubtful that anyone takes a risk except the person who feels a measure of safety in his bones. Part of what it means to be a person in community is to be a person secure enough in love to venture out. Perhaps "training for the Kingdom" is a recovery of the trust that love is there, and in the midst of failing, of trial, and loss, and whatever life brings, that same energizing love will enable us to endure triumphantly.

It is difficult to believe in that love when it remains pure spirit and is not embodied in persons. It was this love that let us shuffle back and forth between the coffee-house service and the familiar blue chapel, which was the place for so much venturing forth. Not only did the old represent a strong base of operation; it blessed and embraced the new, because in the pulpit was a man who was secure enough himself to free others. He had thrilled to the idea of the coffee-house church, and delighted all the way in its growing congregation. So strong was his influence and so deep the devotion to him that with a word or look he could almost have kept that new pulpit from coming into being. He could so easily have made us feel guilty for establishing another worship service alongside his own. Instead, he preached about it and encouraged his congregation, as well as others, to worship there. But mostly he simply rejoiced in its being. This kind of leadership gave to those of us who would have been threatened by the new the encouragement to experiment. The power of our creativity might thrust us out onto some lonely post, but there was a community, however small, from which nothing had the power to cut us off.

It seems so often that we do not let the new come because we have no feeling of a safe place which is ours. We are threatened, for fear the new may hold events in which we cannot participate, people who may exclude us, knowledge which, recognized as truth, must change the way we are, or experiences on which the doors of our own lives may no longer open and which we must turn from lest they evoke our envy. The new can come as a threat in many ways. One of the places we are most vulnerable is at the point of our vocation. This so often becomes the way that we tend to feel secure. I will not be afraid of how well you write unless I am a writer. I will not be afraid of your excellence as a cook, if I am not a chef. I will not be afraid of the ministry of the laity unless I am a minister. Common as this condition is in our competitive, achievement-oriented society, its power to restrict life is not lessened, for it carries the shattering and false word that we may lose our place in the order of things. It makes us unwilling to let go, which is always the precondition for receiving the deeper gift.

A community under Christ embodies the word that there is always a place to stand. It reflects the God who, knowing our finiteness—our need for a place—said, "Have no fear, I go to prepare a place for you." The community holds that Word for the one who does not have it, until it becomes incarnate in him, which means that his confirmation comes from within.

Threat in itself is no enemy that we should rid ourselves of it. In fact, the danger is that we bar the doors lest it come in, when that feeling of threat inside might be a sign of the Presence of God letting us know, if we will listen, that we have put our security in things and places and events and relationships. It is not the threat, but our response to it that is important.

If there was somehow in this community the element of safety, it was not because there was any paternalism around. It sometimes seemed as though our feelings and sensitivities were not well enough protected, and there needed to be more people to smooth the way and give us flat green plains to walk on. The safety was not in protection from "slings and arrows," but in a group of people who, however poorly they might embrace it, had as the basis of their life in Christ an unlimited liability for one another.

In Ecclesiastes it is written, "Two are better than one, because they have a good reward for their toil. For if they fall, one will lift up his fellows, but woe to him who is alone when he falls and has not another to lift him up. Again, if two lie together, they are warm; but how can one be warm alone? And though a man might prevail against one who is alone, two will withstand him. A threefold cord is not quickly broken."

We did not change the order of the chairs in the blue chapel at headquarters, but discussion of it introduced a new dimension into the service. When it was appropriate, the service became a time for the various mission groups to report on where they were and where they thought they were going. Sometimes the scripture would be read by one member of the group, the sermon preached by another, with one or two members adding brief statements on different phases of the mission. Members would also take the offering and serve as ushers. In a way, there was the element of the old testimonial meeting; the new element added was that of a group witnessing to the wonderful works of God as they struggled to live out their call in a small segment of the city. Disappointments, frustrations, and failures overcome were usually spoken of, and this was hope for those of us who were in this kind of experience and wondering if we were going to win our way through to something else. This was the working out of scripture of the one who falls and has another to lift him up. As we watched and listened to each person participating in the service, the variety and richness of personalities and the miracle of their all being bound together in one structure came through. It is said that one picture is worth a thousand words. Before us was that picture. We had heard countless words about the composition of a mission group and the nature of Christian community, but this kind of service was acting it out on a stage, so that we could see the beginning and the end and where the parts fitted in. The drama of it came through in a way that was lost to us in the day-by-day living of it in our own places of mission. The presentations were rarely polished. People simply said what they had to say. Don Hardester gave the sermon on the day the Restoration Corps led the service and began with this explanation for visitors. "I am not Gordon Cosby, or an intellectual, or a theologian. I am Don Hardester, the butcher."

The Sunday service was not only a time when the mission groups could report on what was taking place at their particular posts, it was also an hour when a person feeling a call on his life could sound it for others who might join him in a mission. Always it was a call that had been tested and confirmed at other places in the community, which gave the incentive to issue it to the whole congregation. Sometimes the person would have the sermon that day and give the call within that context. More often it was a short statement that followed the sermon. I think that Martha Harre was the first to stand in the Sunday congregation and invite us to be on mission with her. She said that since the death of her husband twelve years before, she had seen her own widowhood and that of many other women of all ages in a variety of perspectives. She felt that many widows had a wealth of sensitivity and understanding of how to support another human being. "This wealth," she said, "with no outlet, can be easily misplaced and only partially used. The woman, newly alone, quietly, desperately looks around for a meaning in life, growing more ashamed with the passing months to admit the lostness and aloneness that persists." She told how there had grown in her an acute awareness of the possibilities that were open to women who would live deeply into this particular experience of grief. "I believe," she said, "that within this experience is the possibility to learn where one's ultimate security rests, to learn to know one's self and one's true gifts, to learn to minister to a hungry world." She wished to provide a house where psychological, spiritual counseling and other resources could be made available to widows, and gave a call to any who would explore this with her.

These calls issued in the congregation put us in on the beginning of new missions. They also carried for some of us the enormous threat that a person needed in our own mission might go off to the new mission. This could easily happen, for the groups included, besides the core members, those who had not yet been grasped by any call and were trying to discover within the mission group structure the place where they could unreservedly make their commitment.

If the new missions posed a threat, we had to either deal with it internally or learn to live with it, for the mission groups, like the School of Christian Living, were committed to helping associate members discover the place where they could respond at the innermost springs of being. One of the requirements of associate membership was a willingness to examine periodically one's participation in a group. Does this particular framework enable me to be a growing person? Am I moving toward a commitment of my life to this mission? Am I hearing a call to something else? Is there a wakening in me of that which I can sound as call? The authentic mark of a call is that it is sounded from the depths of being, though it may be spoken in a conversation between two or in a church before hundreds. When others make response, then there is a new mission.

If we used the time of Sunday worship as a forerunner of the birth of a mission, we also were aware of the need to use our worship time to give a proper funeral to those missions that had gone down in battle, and sometimes ingloriously. Failure is part of the story of our mission groups, and will be part of the story of any church that is willing to risk itself. The question is, what do we do with our failures? Do we say it isn't so and try to hold the dead up? We have done this also. A group will put their lifeblood into a mission while struggling with the same problems week after week, and year after year. Sometimes they are internal problems, which makes it more difficult because surely we assume we ought to be at that place where any relationship can be worked through. "After all, we are Christians." The implication is that this means to have arrived at a certain place.

The Life Renewal Mission Group, which had as its project the founding of a Residential Center for those in need of emotional support, was strangely enough a group which could not resolve its inner conflicts. Two distinct groups had come together to plan this project—one an intercessory prayer group and one the pastoral counseling group. The intercessory prayer group found its life and integrity centered in the more explicit use of prayer, scripture, and worship. The counseling group in its approach to healing relied primarily on psychological counseling and chose to use religious resources in a less structured way. Each group said it valued and appreciated the viewpoint of the other and wanted to demonstrate in this project the wedding of psychiatry and religion, but somehow the division between the two groups was never really bridged. Despite this, plans went ahead and both groups engaged in the planning and purchase of a house that would be the residential center. As so often happens, the problems emerged with more clarity in the concrete situation. The groups reached an impasse in completing the details of the operation of the house and the philosophy of its ministry. Their approaches differed, and the different viewpoints could not be reconciled.

A group needs to do its grief work when its child is dead, or it is not free to nurture another child. And sometimes the fact that death has happened needs to be symbolized. I was reminded of the place of ritual when I went to the funeral of Lizzie Simmons, who for so many years had cared for us and our church building. Lizzie belonged to three orders, and each order conducted a service. At the head of the coffin stood the person in charge and around it the sisters of the order. Three times the leader called loudly the name Elizabeth Simmons, waiting each time for an answer. Then she turned to the sisterhood and said, "Three times have I called the name of Elizabeth Simmons, and three times there has been no answer. It is obvious that Sister Simmons will not again answer an earthly call. She has replied to another call and listens now to heavenly voices." I wondered if this ritual were in the service to help with the transition from "No, it cannot be" to "Yes, it is." It is fitting also that a dead mission have a service and that the celebrants have time to confess to their Lord, receive forgiveness, and renew their commitment to the mission of the church.

Members of the Life Renewal Mission Group are now vitally engaged in new missions, which makes me think that we bury our dead dreams well. Visitors who talk with us about mission often want to be assured that it is all right to fail, and ask to know about our failures. We guarantee that we have them, but the people who participated in them are usually busily engaged at another point, so that it is difficult in the demands of the new to recall the old with any vividness. The failure of a mission does not mark its people as failures. In fact, failure often taught us more than success could. It taught us to die to some of our illusions about ourselves—to die to some of our "vain strivings." Of course, there was now and then a person so identified with a mission that its failure was his failure, or another was blamed. Above this failure God's accepting word was never heard, and those times we did, indeed, fail!

I remember the poignant statement of a moderator who in a report to the Council outlined the accomplishments of his group in securing a better education program for children in an underprivileged area, and concluded his statement by saying that much work needed yet to be done, but that the Spirit which had given life to the group had moved on. "To continue," he wrote, "after the Spirit has moved on would be to make a mockery of the greatness of the original experience and would hold us in a form which now lacks that vital substance. For this reason, we request the members of the Church of the Saviour to discharge the Mission Group so that its individuals may be released to seek and find again in new forms that same Spirit which binds us to one another as mission to the world."

Perhaps with this a word of caution should be given lest we give up too early. We have never had a mission group in the history of the church which has not had to endure hard times. One moderator, reporting for a group, said, "What we called our 'social phase,' the period when we were nice and polite, lasted about six months. Now we are in that time when everyone is asking 'What is wrong with this group?' I think this is probably a good phase to be in, because when people ask this question something is bound to happen." This has often been the experience—in the valleys of despair when our minds and hearts were sharpened by questions that had a real ache in them we found direction, found a way into the mountains, to have for a season at least the valleys and the plateaus beneath us.

COMMUNION SUPPER

Two nights a week at 6:30 we have a simple supper of bread and cheese and fruit and coffee. No reservations are made. Sometimes a person will decide to stop in on his way home from work. Sometimes we plan to be at the Communion supper on the night our mission group meets. Others drop in just once a month, or not at all. On some nights there are as many as twenty, on others as few as six.

It is never a supper that we go to as attenders. The requirement is that we be participants, prepared to enact a drama together. This means that we will come prepared to extend the "kiss of peace," or—said in another way—we will come prepared to be open to one another, to take the initiative of love with the stranger. In the early community, if the celebrant could not pass the peace, he could not stay for the Communion service. As we ourselves live in community, the reason for this becomes clear. We see how easy it is to say week after week the words that appear in church bulletins and never relate them to one's life. Of course, it is not only the church that has holy words. Social reformers and community organizers with plans for changing the city and no plans to change themselves, wear their piety in secular dress. The truly authentic person in or out of the church reflects in his outward stance the work of his inward parts. There is no cleavage between the outward and the inward. It was this unity that Jesus was after when he said, "If you are offering your gift at the altar, and there remember that your brother has something against you, leave your gift there before the altar and go; first be reconciled to your brother, and then come and offer your gift" (Matt. 5:23, rsv). Be prepared to extend the "kiss of peace" was the instruction given again for the meal at which the Host was Jesus.

The second requirement was that we come to the Communion supper prepared to make an offering out of our day. It could be a symbolic offering of our work—an eraser or a slide rule. It could be a report of what was happening in our own individual life, or in the life of our mission group. It could be God's Word as it came in an event of the day, or a reminder to our community of the covenant under which we lived. It could be a happening somewhere in the world, on behalf of which we gathered. It might be simply our silence offered up upon the Communion table. To make this kind of preparation was to grasp the possibility of living through the day in a different kind of way. The fact that it could be offered up at the Communion meal was to perceive it—to be present to it and therefore a celebrant in it, to understand that there was some relationship between the world and the Communion table, the secular and the sacred.

It is a meal that begins as the Last Supper must have begun, with the serving of food and the finding of places at tables and an exchange of conversation back and forth. Then the short litany with a reading from scripture: "Because we have been at our work today as servants of his Word, I call upon you now to hear that Word." After the words of confession and absolution comes the time of offering. A watch, more often than any other item, is offered as a symbol of the tyranny of time in a person's life. Once it was placed on the table in thanksgiving for the release that had come to a minister, who said, "I am beginning to see that whatever

God calls me to I will have time to do." A young girl placed a city transfer ticket on the table—"For the bus driver this morning who greeted me cheerfully when I was feeling low." A visitor offered his tie clasp, a symbol of his yearning for status and the approval of people. A salesman put his prospect list on the table and another person his wallet. Often we prayed about a difficult relationship in an office or a decision that needed to be made. Always we pray for the people of Vietnam and the leaders of the nation.

Then the words of the institution are said ". . . Take, eat, this is my Body which is given for you. Do this in remembrance of Me." One person at each table takes the bread that had been part of the common meal, breaks and passes it to his companions.

Likewise we take the cup and in the name of Christ pass it to the one at our right saying, "This is the blood of Christ shed for you." From person to person and from table to table the cup is passed, and He who taught us to do this stands in our midst— Emmanuel, God with us.

RETREAT

In 1953 we had purchased Dayspring—175 acres of woods and rolling Maryland countryside. In the years since then new superhighways had brought it within forty-five minutes of our scattered homes in Maryland and Virginia and the District.

Reflecting on the mystery of the whole Body, joined and knit together . . . when each part is working properly (Eph. 4:16), each of our missions at one time or another has had opportunity to support the other. This is usually in ways we never planned. Varied as our missions are, they often become interrelated at the point of their work. As our life took shape around the needs of the inner city, the Dayspring camping area became a summer playground for city children. The retreat area became the place of renewal for all the mission groups.

A mark of sickness in a group is when you hear its members saying, "This little group is wonderful. I love these people, they love me. This is our church. We don't need the rest." We came to recognize this as idolatry of the particular. It is the eye saying to the hand, "I have no need of you." Sometimes the fear of this kind of idolatry has made the church reluctant to send out small task forces, let alone free a whole membership for work in the missionary field. It is easy for a sense of self-sufficiency to take root and grow, especially in a group that is feeling power and moving ahead in its mission. At the very time a group like this can be of help to groups which have a weaker foothold, it disclaims responsibility. Such a group can come to exercise power, but it is not the power of the Spirit. The Holy Spirit is a communicating spirit. Paul advises that we test the spirits. A group on which the Spirit rests is open and communicating. Its members are growing, not only in their belonging to one another, but in their belonging to the whole Body of Christ, and hopefully in their belonging to all of humanity.

There are many groups informally related to the Church of the Saviour. The mission group is distinct from these. Its members are subject to the Council of the church, and are accountable to all the mission groups and facets known as the Church of the Saviour. Together they try to make concrete their belonging to the churches in Washington and the churches in the nation, and in the world. We can never say, "I don't need the rest," for we need all of mankind—all the strange people we don't like, all the people we do not understand. If this concern, however, never takes a specific shape, then we swing to another extreme—the idolatry of the whole. We bask in the lovely glow of being lovers of mankind— saved from loving any specific segment of humanity.

The church must take the risk of sending out small groups. This may mean that instead of giving less attention to the historical/institutional dimension of its life, we may need to give more, lest these groups become separated from the whole and engage in the idolatry of the particular. The church may need to change its institutional forms, but it will always need them for its missions and the nurturing of people in their belonging both to the whole and to the particular. For us the primary forms for this kind of caring have been the School of Christian Living, the worship services, and the retreat program.

The first building at Dayspring, which we put up with our own hands, was the Lodge of the Carpenter. The large living room and a kitchen and dining room made it possible for eighteen persons to be in day-long retreat. The more involved our mission groups became in the outward journey, the more essential it became to give equal attention to the inward journey. In 1961 we had Claude Ford, an architect in our congregation, design overnight facilities for the same number. The building was contracted for and built in the woods behind the Lodge. Each room has a single bed, a washbasin, a desk, two chairs and lamps. On each door is a copper symbol made by the Workshop mission to identify the room. Inside the room are one or two handcrafted items. The windows all look out on woodland.

The retreat group mission is to strengthen the congregation in the life of prayer. Each year it contacts the other mission groups to plan a time of retreat. This group also plans retreats that are open to those who have not yet moved into mission groups. Half of the weekend dates are used by other churches in the Washington area.

Most of the mission group retreats are led by our own members and follow the more classic outline with emphasis on silence. The open retreats are usually led by friends from other church communities and are more on the order of conferences. We do not find many in our own or other congregations who are well acquainted with silence, which means that there are few who can introduce others to this kind of retreat. As we grow in our understanding of silence, we give more emphasis to the classic retreat with its short instruction periods and long stretches of time for meditation. At the meals one of the retreatants reads aloud—usually from a devotional classic.

At one time we had two-day seminars for ministers who wanted to see the missions of the church and test their authenticity for their own situations. We crammed the two days full of dialogue and a rushing from one mission point to another. We even talked a lot about the inward journey, but were so immersed in activity and stimulated by conversation that it remained theoretical—interesting, but not relevant. It occurred to us that we were not emphasizing, and therefore not communicating, the life of prayer which is the basis of our missions. To include an experience with both the inward and the outward, we changed the structure to one of retreat and seminar, and to four days instead of two. Most of the time now is spent at Dayspring except for one afternoon and evening when the retreatants visit the missions and are in conversation with members. The rest of the time is used for retreat, a great part of which is silence. The structure of the retreat with its periods of instruction and meditation is explained on the first night, and most enter willingly into it, though with strong reservations that it can have any meaning.

The church leaders who have been working with the renewal movement for several years are just beginning to receive intimations that it may not come off, if there is not a corresponding inward movement. Commenting on this, John Oliver Nelson, Director of Kirkridge Retreat Center, said to a conference of ministers, "We are a generation which knows how to picket, but not how to pray."

What the ministers at Dayspring begin to discover within the framework of retreat is that the problem of the renewal of the church is a problem within themselves. The seminar discussions had always centered on what to do with unresponsive congregations and denominational structures that resisted experimentation. In contrast, the retreatant is usually a person looking at himself, examining what in him blocks the renewal of the church.

Our own mission groups found that renewal is not something that happens once and can be held on to. A church coffee house needs renewal in its first weeks and certainly in its second year. The retreat program was designed to help with this continual renewal of our lives on which the renewal of the structures depends.

Each retreat is different. You cannot go to one and know what the next will be like. The Council of the church, comprising three staff members and eight elected members, makes retreat once a year. The first time, we used the entire retreat for intercession, but were so unused to the work of intercession that everyone was exhausted when the weekend came to an end. Since then, we use only half the time for intercession and the other half for meditation on what might be the next steps for the church. In our brooding over the church, we are encouraged to give our imaginations wide range—to be willing to let the impossible emerge. The time of sharing is used to present the unlocked store of ideas. We do not attempt to evaluate them or plan how they might be implemented. If an idea takes root, it finds its way onto the agenda of the Council's regular monthly meeting.

Not all retreats have what our skeptical friends call the mystical element. At the other extreme of the retreat of silence was what we came to call our cigarette retreat, though a purist might not dignify it with the name "retreat." This was given for those of us who had struggled for months and even years trying to give up cigarettes. The hope was that we might be able to do it, if we spent the first two days in a retreat-structured situation. There were two requirements for making this retreat: (1) that we bring no cigarettes with us, and (2) that our intentions be serious. The retreat was in the middle of the week, which meant taking time from work, but seven persons came.

We had a lot of homey rules we had picked up here and there for aid and comfort in making this retreat, such as to drink plenty of water, eat much fruit, and take long walks. Unlike the classic retreat, this was one structured to include many times of meeting for short periods of worship, followed by what turned out to be a kind of group therapy session. We never got far from the subject of cigarettes. This was the absorbing, ever-present subject that we explored from all possible angles. We even figured out that as a group we spent about $1,400 a year on cigarettes, which, invested over twenty years, came to some staggering amount. Even $1,400 would have been a great gift to some of our missions, not to mention the help to our personal budgets. When analyzed, however, money was not incentive enough for being on the retreat, nor were any moralistic reasons. Even the specter of death by cancer held little motivating power, which is borne out by the increase in the nation's cigarette consumption since the publication of findings that prove the relationship between smoking and disease. Most of us were there because we had a hacking cough, a headachy cigarette hangover, and milder symptoms which in no way frightened anyone, but detracted from a general feeling of well-being.

The few theological discussions we had on this retreat came about primarily because some were suffering from guilt over devoting a retreat to the problem of cigarette addiction. When we held this problem against the backdrop of Vietnam and other grave issues, it seemed to a few that we were giving our attention to the wrong subject. This got us into a discussion of the place of the "unimportant" and helped us see better how the large decisions of life are determined by the small. The scripture verse given to the group was I Corinthians 10:12-13 (RSV): "Therefore, let anyone who thinks that he stands take heed lest he fall. No temptation has overtaken you that is not common to man. God is faithful, and he will not let you be tempted beyond your strength, but with the temptation will also provide the way of escape, that you may be able to endure it."

Again, this seemed to a few a scripture that should be reserved for times of great stress or tribulation, but it was argued that it had no possibility of serving in those hours unless it was practiced in small things. Our response in the hour of crisis would not be determined by someone giving us a great and appropriate scripture. The runner must be in the small race, if he has the possibility of winning in the big race.

Community was given to us on that retreat and in the days following we called each other to give encouragement and to ask for it, but with all that help, only two out of the seven resisted the temptation that proved too strong. We kept losing track of our scripture, not being convinced that we should cling to it in so small a matter. We forgot that some of us had for twenty years bowed our knee to cigarette counters, left an offering, and received our incense. Not only was the cigarette pack one of our gods, but one on which we heavily depended.

Our failure has not discouraged us. We are ready to experiment with another cigarette retreat—perhaps one which does not center so much on talk about cigarettes. We think one of our mistakes was to talk too much and not give enough time to engagement with God. Not only are we ready to try another cigarette retreat; we have one scheduled on weight control, and plan to have others on such subjects as economic anxiety. No subject has as much power to evoke feeling as money. Perhaps this is because there is no more symbolic commodity in the world, and it is the one that has the most to say to us about who we are and what we hold to be important.

The various kinds of retreat make for a oneness between the mission groups and also interweave our lives with other church groups. In the fall of 1963 the Liturgical Conference, an association of Catholics concerned with the Church's life of worship, met at Dayspring to draft material for modernizing the Mass. The group consisted of nine priests and six laymen. They had not expected the restfulness and beauty that is Dayspring. Carolyn and Tom Hubers and Gloria and Don McClanen, who live at Dayspring, were their interpreters as well as hosts and cooks for the session. Mass was said before Kay Pitchford's bas relief, which covers one wall in the reception room and portrays nine scenes from the life of Christ. The week after the session was over, one of the retreatants wrote to "Friends of Dayspring." "I cannot readily express how much those days of study and celebration of the Eucharist meant to the Liturgical conference. In fact, only time can tell how much our stay there meant to our fellow Catholics and (please God) to the Christian world." We looked back on those days and knew that because of them we were more aware that we had the same Lord. They were days that brought to mind the believers who were amazed that the Holy Spirit had been poured out even on the Gentiles (Acts 10:44).

Retreat has a large part in our individual lives as well as in our corporate life. It is here that one often sees clearly the merging of engagement with self and engagement with God. The story of Bud Wilkinson is like a story out of Acts, and Acts is hard to believe unless you can see it somewhere in modern dress. If Bud appeared the mystical artistic figure, I probably would not write his story, for a part of me would have discounted its message, saying that this is the kind of person temperamentally suited for religious experience. As it is, Bud does not qualify as the type. He is a rugged and earthy kind of man. In the 1930's he was one of the boy tramps of America's depression years, traveling the freights and living in hobo camps. He joined the army at seventeen because to a boy of the Chicago slums the army seemed to offer the only possibility of making something of his life. In 1953 he was an army captain with five years to go to retirement, but the restlessness that had never quite departed was with him again. He was not familiar with the use of words like gifts and destiny, but in his feelings he knew he wasn't using his gifts or following his destiny. Since childhood the field of arts and crafts had beckoned to him, but remained forbidden territory. It loomed again, but still remained out of bounds, nor did he guess that the restlessness in him might be stirred by unfulfilled areas in his life. The internal pressures, however, were enough for him to throw up his army career. He took a job in the field of public relations and used his natural talents for writing and advertising layout to promote a program for the safe transit of packaged goods, but this only ignited the creative urge that had smoldered through the years. By this time he had become a member of the church and moved deeply into its life. Dayspring became for him a place of pondering and wrestling with decision. Here he began to hear the call to be a retreat leader and with it the call to explore seriously the field of arts and crafts. Was it possible that he could be a retreat leader and have art as his tent-making? The person he talked to most about this was his wife, Inez.

I remember a poem read in our chapel—"Wild the dreams, wilder the dreamers." It is one thing to follow a dream when you are one and twenty, and another when it is mid-January and you are forty-six. Bud was forty-six and the snow was on the ground when he reported one morning to the Potter's House Workshop to begin a year's exploration in the field of art. This was the time that he and Inez had agreed to. They would risk Bud's foothold in the world of business and one year of their lives to follow wholeheartedly this part of the inward journey. Since they had no money saved, Inez went to work to support them both. Perhaps this was the biggest risk they took, for it went against all the mores of a culture that was deeply ingrained in them both, and stirred feelings that they would not be able to let go unexamined.

Two weeks after reporting to the Workshop, Bud led a retreat at Dayspring. It was to be a usual weekend retreat beginning at 7:00 on Friday night and lasting through the noonday meal on Sunday. It was snowing again and most of the retreatants did not arrive until 10:30. The late dinner hour and the snow falling outside only added to the expectancy and sense of adventure that enfolded the group. That night Bud instructed them on the nature of retreat and the place of silence in it. He believed unreservedly in retreat as a time "set aside for God." He felt that silence was a gift that we continually disregarded. He believed that the dialogue between God and man can best begin in the silence when, having addressed God in prayer, man waits His reply.

Somehow the unbelievable was communicated to this group.

Bud transmitted his own expectancy—the possibility of an engagement with the One who was Other.

The next day began for him with a deep sense of approval. It was as though God had finally said, "I confirm you as a retreat leader." All day there was an atmosphere of reverence, and a depth in the silence. There was not the resistance one sometimes meets when silence is new to a group and an unspoken language is found to communicate hostility. Confident that everyone was experiencing a real time of retreat, Bud now knew the confirmation of the community in his role as retreat leader.

That night he went to sleep with a feeling of expectancy still in him. At thirty minutes past midnight he awakened abruptly to full consciousness. "It was as though someone had taken me by the shoulder and shaken me. The white light of the stars reflecting from the new snow filled my room, and a voice said, 'You are a potter and you will always be a potter.' "

The following Monday for the first time he tried out the potter's wheel at the Workshop. He had never been on one before. He has scarcely been off one since. All that year he practiced every day for hours on the wheel. His reading program became all the books ever published on pottery. After his study at The Potter's House Workshop, he enrolled in a ceramics class at the Corcoran School of Art in Washington. When he had completed three semesters of study, Richard Lafean, director of the Ceramics Department, said to him, "Bud, you've had enough of classroom instruction. What you need now is the discipline of working and creating for twelve to fourteen hours a day in your own studio."

The basement of the hundred-year-old barn at Dayspring became Bud's studio. It took a month to wash the old stone walls and sweep the caked dirt from the beamed ceiling, but finally it was done. The kiln was installed, and Bud was at work as the potter of Dayspring. To the dedication of his studio he invited those who had played a significant role in his spiritual trek, beginning with his wife and Dorothy Dittmer, the friend who had introduced them to the church saying, "Come and see!" With his words of thanks to the small assembled group, he said, "I know that my vocation is to witness to Jesus Christ as Lord and Saviour—to be, as best I can, God's channel for bringing men into deeper relationship with God. My avocation is potter—one who listens to God as he works—one who creates from the clay that which is useful and beautiful. And, hopefully, one who himself is shaped into something useful and beautiful by the hands of the Master Potter."

Often we are lured from a retreat or the work of Dayspring to stand in the potter's house and watch the potter at his work, and sometimes to wonder what word might be formed in us if we were to listen, quiet and yielded, in the silence.

8

Preparation for Mission

The School of Christian Living is part of the training ground for participation in the mission of the church. The classes, like the mission groups, are structured to make possible those three essential engagements: with God, with others, with self.

Any continuing commentary on the life of this church must give some space to its educational program. Education is a crucial issue of the churches today, and probably the most neglected in the current struggle for renewal.

Because we persist in requiring completion of five courses for membership in the Church of the Saviour, there are some who feel that belonging is "for the elite," and are frank to tell us so. There are others who feel that the requirement is an answer to integrity of membership, but cannot imagine a congregation willing to go to school for several years.

I am reminded of these comments when I attempt to describe our school. It has an atmosphere of contagious excitement, but it also has a quality of disorder in its ordered life. It is a high-pitched disorder at the beginning of the year, into which some calm comes as the year progresses and the gift of Christian community is received here and there. Diversity in temperament, background, and experience among the 150 participants accounts for the churning mood that sometimes comes. Occasionally it is a diversity so great that the classes seem in jeopardy. The mission groups draw the unchurched into the School from varied segments of the city. The churched are there also—Pentecostals who shudder at the name of Tillich sit together with those who are finding inspiration and freedom in the new theology, but not such freedom that their hearts do not beat angrily when someone is unsophisticated enough to say, "Praise the Lord!"

Those with the intellectual approach usually scorn those who lean to the emotional. Those who are eager for mission and have been attracted by the church's involvement in the city fight the disciplined devotional life that is its basis, while others who are attracted by the opportunity to grow in the life of prayer and worship look askance at coffee houses and freedom walks. These are some of the people who find themselves sitting together in the same classroom, often unable to listen to one another. The more aggressive will demand classes tailored to what they feel to be the *real* need. There may be some elite among them, but they are not the "elite" of God. If they have any understanding of Christian community or even ecumenicity, it is of the head and not the heart. When one of the would-be avant-garde asked a young man where he worked, he answered, *Christianity Today.* "Good God!" exclaimed his inquisitor, "What are you doing there?" The young editor quietly replied, "Sir, the question is, what am I doing here?"

One thing is certain, very few enrollees in the School are there to prepare for membership in the Church of the Saviour. Some commute from Baltimore and New York. Some are from other churches in the city. Some would not dream of becoming associated in any permanent way with organized, institutional Christianity. What they have in common—this strange and discordant crew—is an undefined and hidden hunger. If we speak of this in religious terms, we can call it a hunger after God, a hunger to find meaning, to receive one's own unique life as gift.

The fact that this hunger is met in some measure is what enables the students to tolerate each other and withstand the frustrations that are part of the experience. If ever they come to call this hunger by name and recognize it in each other, then, and only then, will they become pilgrims together—a community in Christ.

It is this hunger—after knowing one's own life—to become fully human, that the preaching of the Church ought to uncover and that the new schools of the Church should keep central in their thinking. A recent article reported that almost every major Protestant denomination in the country is involved in a multimillion-dollar effort to develop new program materials for its Sunday schools. But who will teach the material? If we want our children educated we must begin by educating adults, and this not by duplicating courses in religion that can be found in any college, but by giving our hearts and minds to the discovering of what will nurture growth in the adult. Jung says that what we need is schools for forty-year-olds, and he is right if he includes, as it appears he means to do, the thirty-year-olds and the eighty-year-olds. He has a message which the churches in their fight to update the Sunday school need to hear. "It is only in an age like ours," he writes, "when the individual is unconscious of the problems of adult life, or—what is worse—when he consciously shirks them, that people could wish to foist this ideal (educating the personality) onto childhood. I suspect our contemporary pedagogical and psychological enthusiasm for the child of dishonorable intentions: we talk about the child, but we should mean the child in the adult. For in every adult there lurks a child—an eternal child, something that is always becoming, is never completed, and calls for unceasing care, attention, and education."* Jung's work with the sick underlined for him the importance of the childhood years, but it also taught him that far more important than textbooks are the adults in a child's life.

There is no other community besides the church charged to keep a shepherd watch over the "eternal child." This may be why the same judgment that falls on the Church is not directed at other institutions, despite their dehumanizing structures. Surely the fulfillment of its shepherding, pastoring responsibility is the urgent imperative given to the Church today, but it cannot become a

---

* C. J. Jung, *The Development of Personality, Collected Works,* Vol. 17 (New York: Pantheon Books, 1954), p. 170.

pastoring people until care, attention, and education have enabled those who bear the name Christian to set out on their own journey of becoming. This includes a self-conscious awareness that one's belonging to the Church is a belonging to a chosen people, who while in the world are not of the world. We blur the distinction today in our eagerness to be "relevant" and not to offend those who are not of the Church. The charismatic power of the early Church derived from the experience of knowing itself as the bearer of a special message, which still is that "the Kingdom of heaven is within"—the Good News, "You can be who you were intended to be."

It is the sense of its chosenness by God that enables a community to address God, to seek after His word in their history, in the individual events of life, in conversation and dreams and visions. We cannot talk about the Church being in the world today without talking about a community whose life coheres in a Servant Lord. A new positioning of the Church in the world, which all renewal literature asks for, is needed, but this will not convey the new creation. Only a visible community where one can experience the breaking down of the dividing walls within oneself will make witness to a God who calls us out of estrangement and isolation.

As we plan each year for our School of Christian Living, there is usually someone to present the tempting thought that we should break down the classes so that kindred, like-minded spirits can be together. The suggestion is that we put the intellectuals in one class and the mystics in another and devise still other categories for those who do not fit these. Enough of us know, however, that if such a plan were to succeed, the church would have at the heart of its life a heretical structure. It would lose the possibility of being a link in the line of those who demonstrate in their own lives the unity that all men have in Christ. "When one is united in Christ, there is a new world; the old order has gone, and a new order has already begun."

It was to help with the proclamation of this "new order" that we introduced into the curriculum of the School a class in Christian community, or vocation, as it is sometimes called. Gordon Cosby taught the first class. In the course of it a meatcutter was to tell how every day of his life he was forced to cheat customers so that he could keep his job and his family could live. In that class a fastidious professor of economics was to agree with a saleswoman that his disciplines ought to include dirtying his hands once in a while. In that class a plumber heard another say, "I see in you an artist." In that class a brilliant student of theology was to comment, "I can't understand a word anyone is saying."

It was a class which did not attempt to give a formula for Christian community, but somehow enabled the members to experience it and respond in unaccustomed ways, which means that change took place—a new order had begun to emerge.

It would probably be more appropriate to assign to the appendix of this book an outline of the course in Christian community, but I include it here because it clarifies what I am talking about and is suggestive of material which helps a class to be on an inward journey. Gordon says that it is an easy class for anyone to teach because the students do all the work. In one way he is right—only twenty or thirty minutes of each hour-and-a-half session are given to the introduction of new material, which is background for the assignment. The rest of the time the students report what they have discovered as they work with the material from the previous week. Before outlining the content of the classes, I want to emphasize that I don't believe the expectancy and willingness of class members to share their experiences so openly developed only because of the instruction given, but because of the person of Gordon Cosby. He is himself an expectant person. It never occurred to him that this class might not do the assignments or that every member might not have something very important to say. His appreciation and enjoyment of what was going on helped us all to appreciate and enjoy, or at least wonder what it was he was seeing and hearing. "I knew," said one person, "that this was a man of faith, and that he included in it the faith that I could have faith. I became expectant myself, and when I became expectant, things began to happen for me." Another person said, "I would think someone did not have the background to be able to learn. When I realized this was a false judgment, it opened up learning processes in me."

The class began with a reading from *Prayer in Practice* by Romano Guardini,* a writer new to us, but one who has for twenty-five years influenced the Catholic Church in Germany. The

* New York: Doubleday Image Book, 1963.

section read was from the chapter on "Collectedness," which makes irresistible that condition of being "gathered together" which is unfamiliar to most men today, but is the state that enables a man to be present to himself and to others and to God—"the state in which he may when the call comes to him, answer in the words of Moses, 'Here am I' " (Exod. 3:4). Somehow Guardini makes it believable that there is this "mysterious place" into which a man may step to get hold of himself, and which even more than a "place" is a "centre of power."

The assignment given that first night was to continue reading Guardini's book, and every day for five minutes practice reaching a state of inner attention. We were to write not more than one paragraph on the experience.

The papers were read at the next meeting of the class. I cannot remember any which bore witness to finding a quiet place within. Instead they told of unrest, distractions, and an inability to empty one's mind of the shifting outward scene for even five minutes. "Every time I tried to center down in myself," said one woman, "I thought of something I wanted and how I would get it." "I kept thinking," said a man, "of things at work I had to do." Most of us learned, not about quiet, but about our own pervasive condition of unrest.

The second assignment was to read the first chapter of this book and note the times during the week when we were aware of being on that popular highway—the way of the crowd. This was to give us an opportunity to struggle with the concept of being separated from one's real self. We were also to note those times in which we were aware of being present to ourselves and to God and others— walking the "narrow way."

It was again a difficult assignment because the class was working with material which was new for many and which was to help make us aware of the world within and above, and without. Gloria McClanen was one of those who volunteered to share her paper. A discussion of it helped clarify for some what this being "present" was all about. Gloria and Don McClanen live in the farmhouse which is at the entrance of our Dayspring Farm and retreat center. Here they give direction to many of the activities that center at Dayspring. At this post they are subject to the unreal as well as the real needs of a congregation. To Dayspring are also brought the assorted demands of friends from other congregations.

Gloria told the class about a knock at her door that had come the night before. She had opened to an exuberant, effervescent woman who explained that she was from a church in Chicago. She was late arriving at the farm because she and her family, who were out in the car, had been sight-seeing all day in Washington. Her minister, however, had told her that she would find overnight accommodations at Dayspring and so they had confidently arrived. She assured Gloria that they would be no trouble, since they would depart early in the morning. When Gloria got the opportunity, she explained that the retreat center was used exclusively for retreat purposes and that there was a group retreating there. The woman did not grasp this information and went on to state her needs, as well as to exclaim profusely about all the wonderful things she had heard about the Church of the Saviour. "I was aware enough of my own feelings," said Gloria, "to know that I was angry at this sight-seer for intruding on the few hours in the week that belong to my family. At the same time, I wanted to live up to her image of a 'good Christian,' and began to turn over in my head how we might put them up in the farmhouse for the night. When my mind began to move in that direction, I became aware of my mother listening in the next room to our conversation and sending me the message, 'You are always wearing yourself out for strangers who are taking advantage of you.'"

The story seemed to illustrate a conflict which is not uncommon on the "broad highway." We want to please the authority figures in our lives, we want to conform to what the world thinks is "gracious," "polite," "Christian," and we want also to be true to our own feelings. But how does one trust one's own feelings, especially when they are angry? Is it possible in the midst of being pulled one way and then another to move into that state of collectedness where the issues can be clearly seen; where, free from outside pressures, we can discover the way which is ours to go? In other words, could Gloria be present to herself and, gaining awareness of the forces that were playing on her, push past them to that "mysterious place" from which she could make reply to this stranger as "one who speaks with authority?" What Gloria said to the class that night was that she was aware of being caught between what the woman wanted her to do, what her mother wanted her to do, and what she thought the church would want her to do, and that in the midst of these conflicting voices she had found a voice from within to obey. She was uncertain that it was God's, and she was uncertain that she was ever present to that woman.

This assignment was repeated, and as other papers were shared it became clearer that none of us was going to operate from any quiet center unless we became more practiced in getting there. If we could not still our minds for five minutes in the morning when the closet door was closed, we were not going to be able to do it in the midst of the day's traffic.

The fourth assignment given to the class was to list those disciplines which each member felt would help him to grow—to be a person "present"—and which we would also want to practice living by for the next weeks of the class. It was suggested that the disciplines include a five-minute recollection exercise. The assignment of listing our disciplines, like every other, was shared with the class, who freely gave their thoughts on it. Though members had been cautioned against laying upon themselves too heavy a burden, most ignored the warning. It was this part of the disciplines that came in for most correction by the group. We were able to see the impossible goals that others had set for themselves, and this helped us see that our own were equally unrealistic. The young and overconscientious worker in the slums was told to include in his disciplines at least one evening and possibly a day for his own recreation. It was felt, however, that a few had been so easy on themselves that they could hardly be serious about the Christian life. Class time was taken for each of us to ponder our disciplines in silence and make any revisions that we felt were indicated by the class discussion.

The fifth assignment concerned another important area of life in community—the exercising of one's own gifts. Gordon explained that if we were to be lovers of mankind and of men in particular, it would be necessary to exercise our own gift—our own charisma. He said that this was a matter of finding out what we really want to do and of doing it, which is quite different from doing our duty or what is expected of us. It did not mean living out of a spirit of "oughtness." "It is the faith," said Gordon, "that God has called us—each of us—into being to play a part in His cosmic drama, and that hints of what this part is come to us through our deepest longings and desires. What we deeply want to do is often what we ought to do. What we think we *ought* to do and feel compelled to do may not be God's intention at all."

The assignment was to work with the question, "What are my gifts?" It was suggested that those who had difficulty naming their gifts, or who were aware of so many that they had become dabblers—never singling out one, and therefore never developing any fully—might be helped if the question were rephrased "If you could do anything you wanted to do, what would you do?"

As I have mentioned elsewhere, this assignment always engenders guilt feelings, and makes it evident that part of what deters us from discovering our own gift is that it seems selfish to focus to this degree on ourselves. Guilt also seems a part of realizing one's potential. A person answering a call is singled out of the crowd. He is overturning the established order of things. This was the underlying note of most papers.

Gordon stressed again that one of the first steps in loving another is to let God call into being our own unique charisma. He explained love as an event in which we give ourselves to another, and that we do not give ourselves to another if our own essence, what we are intended to be, is not actualized. "If our own potential is blocked," he said, "and has found no creative channels in which to flow, then what we feel in the presence of another is envy. We may not recognize it as envy—only a perplexing pain or deadness. We will have no praise of another—no joy in another. Instead, we will turn away and in subtle ways seek to destroy the other. This is why we cannot get on with the business of loving unless we are discovering our own gift."

The sixth assignment was to write a paper on what we felt to be the gifts of one other class member. The seventh assignment was to write a paper on what factors in our lives had blocked the realization of our gifts and what had encouraged their realization. Both assignments were to help us uncover our talents, but also understand what nurtured them, so that one day we might belong to a community whose task was not only the exercising of its own gifts, but calling forth the gifts of others.

The eighth assignment was to consider the risks that we were

prepared to take to realize our gifts. This assignment was to enable
the class to understand that one does not enter into one's own
unique charisma without risk-taking. One never discovers who one
is without constantly taking risks—the risks of the loneliness of
exposure, of many wrong turns, or losing one's security; of forfeit-
ing the confirmation of friends. There would be risk all along the
way. It is not a matter of taking one risk and by this step freeing
oneself from risk-taking. A person committed to realizing his full
potential—committed to growing into the fullness of his humanity
—will always be taking risks. It is also very uncertain that we can
become ourselves in all of our uniqueness without knowing anxiety, for it involves becoming conscious of what we have been
unconscious of, which means eating forbidden fruit. "We will not
often take that step," said Gordon, "unless we learn to be present
to Him who issues the call to this kind of adventure, and lets us see
in Himself the example of One who is utterly and absolutely free."

The next session covered briefly the three types of relationships
we need, if we are to be people growing. We need those who are
further along the way, who give us hints of where we are and raise
the question of where we are going—what the next step might be.
They may be teachers or counselors, or, when we are without
these, books. Then we need those who are our peers—fellow pilgrims with whom we share the day-by-day events of our life in
Christ, the discoveries we make, the places where we are challenged, our discouragement, our hope; brothers who hold us accountable, who remind us of our covenant relationship; brothers
who mediate forgiveness. And thirdly, we need those who are not
so advanced as we—a little flock which is ours to tend and nourish. "All these relationships," said Gordon, "are utterly necessary
to our spiritual development, but the one I want us to look at in
this class is the one of being shepherds, because it is at this point
most of us will feel the most hesitancy or timidity. We will feel that
it is pretentious for us to be guides to others at the point of their
life in Christ."

He then outlined three reasons why we shrink back and commented briefly on each.

1. *A sense of unworthiness.* "Who am I to think of doing this?"
The feeling is that the shepherd role is concerned with the holy and

should be left to the professionals—some special class of people whose special business it is. In every other realm we are willing to share what we know even if our knowledge is most limited. We are willing to advise our friend on how to keep his lawn in good shape, or the kind of car he should buy; or teach him what we know about bridge or golf, though it may not be very much. But when the subject moves into things spiritual, then we shrink back. "I know very little about prayer and therefore I am unwilling to share even the little I know."

2. *Fear of involvement.* It is one thing to give a little spot help here and there, have a little conversation on the meaning of death or sickness, but to self-consciously assume the role of spiritual director is something altogether different, for this puts us in the position where another can call on us a month or a year or two years from now. Was not von Hügel the spiritual director of many for a lifetime?

3. *A sense of the impossible.* Every person is so different. How can we possibly know what is right for another? We don't even know what is right for our own children, not to mention ourselves.

"Be a spiritual director?! From this we shrink back," said Gordon, "exclaiming, 'Who am I to do this?' How can we exclude from our lives a willingness to help others in their loneliness and hunger when there are thousands upon thousands to whom no official organization will minister. There will be thousands upon thousands of others who will be open to no professional when they will be open to you."

The assignment was to read von Hügel's four qualifications for a spiritual director as given by Douglas Steere in his introduction to the *Spiritual Counsel and Letters of Baron Friedrich von Hügel** and then to meditate on the following:

1. What feelings get evoked in me when the call to be a spiritual director is extended? What did Christ mean when he said, "Feed my sheep?" Who did he mean to do it? and when?

2. Meditate on your life at the point of the four qualifications von Hügel gives for a spiritual director.

3. Do you get any hints of whom your flock might be?

* New York: Harper & Row, 1964, pp. 10-13.

It took two sessions to consider all the feelings evoked by this assignment. There was some violent objection to the use of the term spiritual director, though no one found a more satisfactory one. There was also raised the question of the eager beavers—those who feel quite capable and reach out to take on anyone who comes within their orbit. Said one person, "I had a hard time extracting myself from one of these would-be counselors." Most of us were aware of this type of person, and Gordon responded by saying that if we were out corraling a flock, we had better be wary. "The need in the world today is so great that you won't have to worry about gathering in your sheep. When you are open and willing, and ready, the hungry and bleating lambs of God will sense a shepherd in their midst and come milling around. You will know then what Christ meant when he said 'The fields are white unto harvest.' " And then Gordon added, "It is my conviction that the roadblock in the whole renewal movement is the lack of shepherds."

The hunger Gordon spoke about was witnessed to by members of the class, most of whom said, "I can't be a spiritual director, I need one." Gordon emphasized again the necessity for assuming this responsibility for another if we were to know any vivid sense of God's presence. "It is so basic," he said, "that unless we deal with this call in our lives, we will reach a point beyond which we cannot go. Feeding and tending others is central to our life as Christians."

For the ninth assignment, we again turned to Douglas Steere's introduction to Baron von Hügel's *Spiritual Counsel and Letters,* in which he gives us the essence of eighty pages from von Hügel's *Mystical Element of Religion.* "Here a full and fruitful religion is described as containing a creative tension between the mystical or emotional element, the historical or institutional element, and the intellectual or scientific."* We knew, with Douglas Steere and von Hügel, that "the spiritual guide who will speak to the soul's real need must teach it the place of each of these elements in a full religious diet or ration." Also, we knew that each of us in his life leaned toward one of the three. It was rare when you found in one person these three elements operating in any kind of tension with

* P. 7.

each other. There was also usually little awareness of any need to develop the weak areas. When theologians were invited to visit us, the intellectuals turned out, but when someone was speaking on the mystical, those who came were the ones in whom this side was already highly developed. Not only do we continue to develop one side of ourselves at the expense of others, but we hold our way to be superior and write off those who hold to another. Personality or temperamental differences, as much as doctrinal, are a divisive element in Christian community.

"Within all three dimensions," Gordon told the class, "we are to help one another grow into the fullness of the stature of Christ. If a person is more highly developed at the point of the mystical/emotional, we are to help him develop at the point of the intellectual/scientific. If he is weak at the point of the historical/institutional, we must confront him with the Christ of history and the Church."

The assignment was to decide which of these three elements was most developed in our own lives and which the most neglected. The next week was again an alive time of sharing. As in all the other sessions, we were dealing with the content of our own lives, and this is seldom found to be dull material.

The last assignment was to reexamine the disciplines we had made in the early weeks of the course and to share any understanding or feelings that had emerged as we struggled to keep them.

The class touched on five themes which are basic to preparation for any mission.

1. The need to develop an interior life, if we are to be people who are present:

2. The need to discover and to exercise our own gifts, if we are to be a celebrating people, open to life;

3. The need of disciplines for the realization of any potential;

4. The need to know ourselves, if we are to be a people growing; and

5. The need to be shepherds, if ever we are to cross that intangible line to where the emphasis of our life is more on giving than on receiving.

Other classes, with their different emphases, bring us to grips with the same issues, but in utterly different contexts. For all of their concreteness and their grounding in the raw material of every day, they are classes which deal not with earthly things but things supernatural. They deal with love and what it means to be free. They point toward Jesus Christ, the One without whom no man becomes fully free. "If then the Son sets you free, you will indeed be free."

9

The Covenant Community

Jim Alrutz was a member of The Potter's House mission and working on his Ph.D. in international relations when he began to reflect on the real meaning of life in community. As part of the Crossroads Africa program he had helped refugee students build their own school. He had been a leader of similar work communities in Ghana and in Mexico. He was ready to work all his life for community between peoples and nations; but first he wanted a deeper experience of it in his own life. As he talked with friends he found others with his own eagerness, and together they began to think of the possibility of living in an intentional community. This was the spring of 1964.

Through that summer a dozen young men and women met to worship together and to envision what the community might be— its structure and its disciplines. At first they shared their hopes, and then their fears. As they talked about a corporate mission, it became clear that the covenant they were forming meant not only that they would give up their present living arrangements, but also their jobs. Some were students who would have to interrupt their education. Some were concerned about what their families would think. It was a summer of uncertainty, of questions and searching. But there was an evening in that summer when they gathered in a basement room of the church, and in the midst of their doubts there was the sense of the numinous. "It was almost," said one of them, "as though there was something between us and at our center which affected the way we related to each other. We all felt it. It did not change our self-centeredness or take away our anxieties about what we were trying to do, but it affirmed us. After that, prayer became more a posture and attitude, rather than a deed."

In those summer weeks the primary discipline was to pray each day for one person in the group and the emerging community. At the end of July, it was agreed that another month should be given to exploration, and the first of September was set as the time of decision when they would either begin their life together or disband.

In their early meetings they had considered a monastic kind of order off in some countryside, but as they talked about the kind of growth they wanted for their own lives, it seemed to them that to be in "Christian community" meant also to be on mission, and to be on mission as the Church meant to be in community. The practical problem was whether to concentrate first on mission or on community.

The natural response was to think of what they might do—what social or economic or political change they might bring about. "What great work can we accomplish?" Should they follow their inclination to tackle this question first or should they devote the greater part of their time to discussing their life with one another, trying to learn what it meant and what it could mean to belong to one another—not only to *do* together but to *be* together? In retrospect, Jim Alrutz said, "I am grateful that in the early stages of our development we chose to concentrate on being and becoming a community. I am now convinced we could not have taken the responsibility of our mission as it finally developed until we had taken seriously our responsibility to those in the group. We had to risk being ourselves with each other before we were ready to risk ourselves with those we did not know—the people to whom we would find ourselves on mission."

The doors of the Coffee House Church open at 10:30 for the Sunday service which begins at 11:00 a.m. There is seating for only seventy persons and many have to be turned away each week. The line shown here had formed by 10:15.

Worshippers become intensely involved in the dialogue following the sermon. They are free to comment on the sermon, or take issue with it. Participants in the worship stay to talk long after the service has been concluded.

Gordon Cosby serving as dishwasher at The Potter's House. Two hundred or more guests in an evening gives high priority to the job. If dishes pile up, volunteer staff are subject to duty at this station.

David Bourns, of the Covenant Community, sits on the back steps of a house on Seaton Place, and engages in conversation with three friends.

Bishop Reed stops to greet Jim Alrutz of the Covenant Community.

Lynn Trout and Margy Gurney, members of the Covenant Community, with pre-school children.

In a 100-year old barn at Dayspring, Bud Wilkinson has his studio.

Gordon Cosby at Dayspring, the Church of the Saviour's retreat center for contemplation and re-creation.

Gift House, another mission venture of the Church of the Saviour, is an outlet for handicrafts.

As they talked, they discovered that they wanted to be in the inner city with the poor. They felt that the essential tasks would be to listen, to learn, and to give themselves—to be neighbors in a society that cannot afford the luxury of neighbors. Hopefully, as they themselves tried to be neighbors, there would be created the milieu that "would allow others to become and to do."

When they began to think of an area in which to locate, they felt drawn to the Adams Morgan section of northwest Washington. The Potter's House and the Workshop were on its main thoroughfare, but in the streets behind lay some of the worst poverty pockets in Washington. The Potter's House had been used for neighborhood meetings, which had put them in touch with some of the people in that area. This is how they came to know Bishop Marie Reed, who became their friend and counselor. Bishop Reed's church was in her own house on Seaton Place. Her flock was the neighborhood, and for them she had learned her way around in the political structures of the city. She knew how to handle landlord problems and get the garbage picked up. She held that decent housing and food and education were basic rights of children, and she moved among the poor and the rich communicating that message. When she spoke to members of the community, she told them she wanted the children of her block to learn to read and write. The public schools knew little of the needs of wounded Negro ghetto children, and expecting them to have middle-class vocabularies and experience, wounded them further because they did not measure up to "average" performance. When the group said they would like to explore working with the children, Bishop Reed agreed to get the mothers together to talk with David Bourns, the group's moderator.

Eighteen mothers came to that first meeting. Most of them were strangers to each other and would not have been there but for the persuasive powers of the Bishop. In discussing the needs of the street, they seemed anxious to give David the answer they sensed he wanted. They were accustomed to white people asking questions, and quite certain that genuine answers were not expected of them. David became aware that when he asked something in a positive way, all gave a confirming Yes. If he suggested a possible program or asked a question in a negative way, everyone said No;

if his presentation was neutral, a hush desended upon the room.

Over the weeks of the summer the group continued their conversations with the Bishop and with mothers in the Adams Morgan area, and the more they talked the more evident it became that the important concern was a chance for the children to learn. "In a sense," said David, "they called forth our gifts. Margy was already a teacher, and the rest of us were in the process of being educated and might one day be teachers."

It began to seem possible to them that they could have a school for three- and four-year-olds, but their confidence was shaken when they read about the many experimental programs being developed for underprivileged children. Aware that they were not equipped with knowledge of elaborate training aids and not yet realizing how long it takes for research programs to be implemented, they went to see the Bishop. Her reply then, as it would be again and again when they were feeling inadequate, was "forget about whether you are doing it right or doing it wrong. We don't need sophisticated stuff. We just need people who will be here and work with us."

By the end of the summer the purpose of the community was defined in these words:

> The Community is to exist in order to build itself in Christ, having at bottom the task of growing in Him and teaching those a part of it something of the meaning of giving themselves to the common service of God. Basic to this will be the acts of common life, commitment to a common rule, and commitment to that community posture, which, in the words of *The Rule of Taize,* "might render it and those individuals a part of it more available."

The name they gave to the experiment was "The Covenant Community." Out of the twelve who explored it through the summer, by September four had committed themselves to it for a year. They were Jim Alrutz, David Bourns, Margy Gurney, and Lynn Trout. David was working at a government agency and participating in the Church of the Saviour as part of an intern program with Union Theological Seminary, New York. Margy was teaching in a Maryland Junior High School, and Lynn was working at the FBI to earn money to finish college. All were under twenty-five, and all, with a reckless but contagious faith, had given up their jobs.

The first thing they did was go in search of a house in Adams Morgan. David found it on Seaton Place—the street they had so often visited. Not only was the house empty, it was condemned. Its windows were broken, its doors absent, and its cellar full of water, with rats floating on top. David described it as "having character." The landlord agreed to rent it to them for $90 a month, with the first two months' rent free if they would put it in acceptable condition. They signed the contract and went to work.

It was this jobless work crew of four that appeared before the Council of the Church of the Saviour to describe Seaton Place, with its row of 55 houses and 76 living units. At that time the children of Seaton Place numbered 246. "Up to ten at night," they reported, "the street looks like a playground."

They planned to begin their day together on Seaton Place with breakfast and the morning office at 7:40, and close it at 11:00 P.M. with evening prayers. Their Rule, which they were still defining, included a total of three hours of prayer, worship, and study each day. Initially, their organized program would consist of a preschool for every three- and four-year-old on the block and a tutoring program for students of all ages.

The major part of their $12,000 budget was for the preschool program. Their plan as a community was to live as simply as possible. The food allowance they budgeted for themselves each day was $4.12, or $1.03 each. They were able not only to live within this amount, but also to provide for a stream of dinner guests.

When one of our more cautious members questioned them about their boldness in giving up jobs before they were assured of sufficient money, they responded that they were prepared to find other jobs if need be, but that this would greatly limit the time they could give to the children and probably make a preschool impossible on a full-time basis. St. Margaret's Episcopal Church, like our own church, was close to the area, and had already responded with a pledge of $3,000. More money was needed, but they were moving out with the faith it would come. Their primary request was for the encouragement, support, and participation of the larger Christian community.

As our Council discussed the mission presented by this enthusiastic group, no one asked whether or not the project could succeed. We knew enough of their weaknesses, as well as their strengths, to have grave misgivings at this point, but the question was not one of success or failure. The question was whether the structure described was one in which four young people could grow and come to know about commitment—being persons in community. The answer was a thoughtful and quiet Yes, for all those on the Council were experienced enough to know that the precious gift of community is costly. It was agreed that Mary and Gordon Cosby would be with them for a meal once a month and help them choose a spiritual director. Bill Shiflett, as minister of missions, was appointed the official liaison. The $1,500 resting in the Church of the Saviour checking account was designated to go to the new community; this left us again without cash—a state so familiar that to some it seems more comfortable, though others still view it with unease.

The Covenant Community continued repairing and painting the house. Their first caller was a bright-eyed four-year-old by the name of Sylvester, who was to be their ever-present companion. When they ate their first meal seated on the basement floor, Sylvester was there to share it. Whenever there was a knock on the door, it was more often than not Sylvester. By his very steadfastness he came to have a special place in their household. He communicated acceptance when they needed it, and they were probably to him the refuge he needed from his own crowded house.

Sylvester was followed rapidly by Pee-wee, Fat Daddy, Stinkey, Boo Boo, and a host of children who seemed to greet their coming as a great and wonderful happening. There was no end to their excitement. They ran countless errands and helped in odd little ways. Because they were so undiscriminating and accepting, the children became the mediators between the anxious four and the not-so-trusting adults on the block. At first, the Covenant Community was amazed that these children were so warm and responsive. But they began to discern that the reason was the hunger of a child for the recognition of his presence; that he had a name, and the hope that you might be the golden person who would say that name.

In addition to the children, there were always small clusters of men standing around on the street. It was DB who came as emissary to look in on them those first days. Gifted with words and always vociferous, he stood in the doorway commenting on a range of subjects, from Faust and Dorian Gray to Japanese photography and house painting. Margy looked up from her own painting to say, "Why don't you give us a hand?" DB thoughtfully surveyed the room and shook his head, "No, too light—I'm a Rembrandt man, myself."

Another friend was Rudy, who had been a saxophone player. When his lip started to go he hocked his saxophone to pay a neighbor's rent. Rudy was the wise man of the street—the counterpart of the village philosopher. His store of knowledge was a never-ending source of astonishment to them. The children knew him as Mr. Rudolph and were attentive to his words, which were meant to encourage. "Bonita, I like pretty girls and you are a pretty girl, but if you do not have a clean face, I will not like you."

If Sylvester, DB, and Rudy, according to the way of each, gave them welcome in those first days, the police did not. They came with the stern advice to leave. "It's a bad block. You'll stir up trouble." Probably Lynn, who was just nineteen, took these words most seriously. For a long time they made her feel unsafe. She and Margy were rooming at our headquarters building on Massachusetts Avenue, but from early morning to late at night they were at Seaton Place. As the weeks went by, however, she lost her fear of the street and began to feel more protected there than anywhere in the city. It became strange to look back to the time when Seaton Place had seemed so menacing. It was not that there was no violence there, but she began to trust that it was not going to touch any of them. More than this, she discovered that she was not the only one who had to grow in trust of her neighbors. Her neighbors had to grow in their trust of her. It had never occurred to her before that others might find her a threatening presence.

When the work of the house was finished, Jim and David moved in, along with an odd assortment of beat-up furniture they had collected, including a spineless single bed in which Jim slept. David had promised to fix it, but he never found time, and the bed became known as "the nest."

Established in their new home, Jim and David were able to give their full attention to the preschool. In search of classrooms, they had visited all the churches in the neighborhood and inspected every vacant building, but had found nothing that would meet District requirements. With eight precious weeks already gone, they decided to start a "bootleg kindergarten" in their own house. They began with two classes of ten children—one meeting in the morning and the other in the afternoon. Margy was the senior teacher and Lynn the assistant. Despite the fact that they had spent four months studying preschool projects, "That first day," Lynn reported, "we looked at each other with 'What do we do?' written all over our faces. We just had to play it by ear."

The picture-word association cards used for privileged children did not work, but they made up their own cards, using magazine pictures of things familiar to the children. They also learned to let them act out plays. In the early days, the children were sober and silent—but after several weeks, Margy and Lynn began to observe them having little conversations with each other. "It was fascinating to watch them," said Lynn. "All of a sudden they seemed like grownups gathered in small groupings to talk." There was one small boy who always wanted to tell what he had dreamed. Soon he could not say, "Last night I dreamed . . ." without the others clamoring to tell theirs. They never tired of telling dreams, which were often dominated by monsters, and "a rat eating me."

It became increasingly evident that rats were an integral part of the life of Seaton Place. One afternoon Margy sat reading to Rickey and Inez *Whistle for Willie,** which is the story of a city child who on a winter day made a snowball; when he went into the house he put it in his coat pocket to save. "That evening," said Margy, "he looked for the snowball in his pocket, and what do you suppose had happened to it?" They said together without an instant's hesitation, "A rat ate it."

Finding books that related to the children was one of the many problems. Each week the press released scores of new books about the poor, but no books for the children of the poor. A volunteer mother who worked with the children knew, however, that she had found one in the picture story of *The Lion and the Rat,*** when a

* Ezra Jack Keats, *Whistle for Willie* (New York: Viking, 1964).
** Jean de La Fontaine, *The Lion and the Rat* (New York: Watts, 1964).

child, pointing to the cover, said, "Oh, I know him. He lives in my house." One of the ways the teen-agers entertained themselves was by chasing rats with sticks and bricks. Some of their elders did the same, and to the fastest rat on the block they had given the name Speedy Gonzales.

One evening David sat on the steps with Elbows, who was fingering a knife in his boot and threatening to even the score with a man who had stabbed his friend. "I'll get him tonight," he said. After they had sat talking for an hour, Elbows invited David into one of the houses. They went down into a basement room where the only light was the big eye of the TV set. They joined the others who were watching an old movie, but Elbows was restless and wandered into the kitchen. When he came back he had another knife. "David," he said, "did you ever hear about Speedy Gonzales? Tonight you'll have a chance to see him. It's about time for him to appear."

Except for the TV, five minutes went by in silence, and then David heard a scratching inside the wall, "Sh-h-h-h," said Elbows, "it's Speedy."

It was obvious to David that it really was a rat scratching and running back and forth in the wall. With the handle of his knife Elbows pounded on the wall. Inside the wall there was a scurrying, and Elbows chased after it. Finally there was no sound, and the eyes that had turned from the TV to watch the drama in the room drifted back to the story on the screen.

"He's too smart," said Elbows. "Speedy Gonzales will not be out tonight. He's the fastest rat on Seaton Place, but he's the smartest, too, and he knows I'd get him tonight."

In those early months a new member was added to the Covenant Community. Walter Hardesty was astonished to find himself there and bound by a covenant to live under disciplines he had never before even considered for himself. He had talked briefly to members of the community in July, but had left soon after to campaign in Florida as State Coordinator of the Young Citizens for Johnson. All his energies went into the election, and when it was over he found himself in a period of great despair—"like nothing I had ever known before." Driving back from Florida to Washington seemed burdensome, there was no feeling of being headed for anything. Not until he had arrived and looked in at the Church of the Saviour had he begun to sense that Washington was where he should be. He was not a Christian, but in a peculiar way the church community was his community.

Walter had never worked in the field of education, but for a long time it had interested him. He was impressed with the importance of reaching children at an early age. When he heard that the Covenant Community was embarked on a preschool program, he went down to Seaton Place to see how things were going. That first day he just visited with the kids on the street, who as usual gave the stranger in their midst a warm welcome. Later Walt talked to Jim Alrutz and Jim invited him to observe the classes held in the house. Fifteen volunteers from St. Margaret's and the Church of the Saviour were assisting in the school, which had been expanded to include forty children. Lynn and Margy now had separate classes. Twenty children came on Monday, Wednesday, and Friday, and twenty on Tuesday, Thursday, and Saturday. Through the weeks when Walter was making his visits to the community he felt a growing openness. Scripture came alive for him, and he began to write his own commentary on St. John. He described it as "a period of being passive and yet responsive to the—Holy Spirit, if you want to call it that." He had explored cautiously with the four the possibility of membership in the community, but still, when the decision was made, he was startled to find himself actually there—"calling myself a Christian among Christians and committed to Seaton Place. It was as though I had waked up in the middle of a dream. I didn't know how it looked from outside, but from inside it looked mighty like a miracle. Afterwards I read William James and found that he described the experience that I had been through and gave it a name—so I allowed as how I had been converted."

While the school went on in their house, Jim and David kept up the search for legitimate quarters. After exhausting possibilities in the immediate neighborhood they talked to Randy Taylor, Minister of the Presbyterian Church of the Pilgrims. Randy invited them to a congregational meeting where they presented their story. When Randy proposed that the Sunday-school classrooms be used during the week for the preschool, the congregation agreed. With

the approval of District authorities, the school moved into its lux-
urious new quarters and began its official life. Since it was too far
for the children to walk, an Episcopal diocese which learned of the
project donated a 1948 bus. Jim became the bus driver and Walter
the new teacher. A grant from a local foundation and other contri-
butions not only assured the budget of the little community but
gave them enough to hire Ilene Detlor, a professional preschool
teacher.

The mothers agreed to form a club and immediately elected
Shirley Williams as their president. There was only nominal attendance at club meetings unless fifteen minutes before time the
Covenant Community team flew from house to house, rounding up
the members with "Hurry! We're having a meeting!" Once the
meeting was under way, the mothers never tired of hearing about
their children and what was happening in the preschool. They even
began using some of the time to make aprons for the children, and
at Christmas they sent a gift of money to the children of Junior
Village. Since a number of the mothers of Seaton Place were on
welfare, the gift would have been difficult for Welfare Department
investigators to understand and would have made them anxious
about their own role in protecting the interests of taxpayers. Erich
Fromm would have understood, however, for he has written that
the real deprivation of the very poor is that they cannot give. And
Jesus would have understood, too, since He said that giving was a
matter of life itself.

The Covenant Community celebrated Christmas on the street.
With the help of the children, they swept the vacant lot beside
them clean of glass and trash and cans, and placed in the middle of
it a tall and shapely Christmas tree—the first tree ever to stand on
Seaton Place. They decorated it with tinsel and lights and paper
ornaments the children had made in school. Everyone said the tree
would be gone by morning, but it stood in gaudy splendor for five
whole days.

Each day revealed the courage of the street; the warmth and
grace of its people in the face of sometimes overwhelming odds.
Need opened upon need. Continually perplexed by the problem of
how to deal with it, and often weary in body, the little community
held to their purpose to live on the street as "be'ers" of the Word,

as well as "doers." To this end they had formed their disciplines—
that they might embody a "style of life."

Guided by the Taize Rule, they had chosen David their Prior
and had given him the authority to make decisions, thus making it
a discipline to abide by those decisions. These concerned such
matters as time spent away from the community or changes in
their program or household schedule. The group arrived at many
of its conclusions together, but where there were differing opinions,
or the matter was not large enough to come before the whole
community, David had the authority to act.

In the area of money they agreed to limit themselves to only
necessary expenditures. Jim was the keeper of the books and at
this point they were accountable to him.

Throughout the year they maintained and worked with the discipline of silent breakfasts and half-hour morning worship services
led by each of them for one-week periods. For two hours each
week they had group Bible study. Each day also included an hour
and a half for individual meditation. This was harder to keep than
the corporate disciplines. It was too easy to feel their fatigue and
take the chance to sleep.

Probably the primary discipline was that of trying to commit
themselves in terms of spirit, resources, and time, to one another
and to their common effort. While there were days when they felt
they could not have made it without each other, and this discipline
posed no problem, there were also days when they thought life
would be sweeter if they were to see the last of the brethren. They
found that the brokenness and estrangement on the street was the
same brokenness and estrangement they found in themselves. The
very maintenance of their household created dissension between
them. They could get furious over small unrecorded expenditures.
They would agree to do better, and then they would not. They
could get all riled up over being told how a meal was to be cooked.
They accused one of being fanatical about keeping the house clean
and another of being a sloppy housekeeper. But probably the
graver problems were those on a deeper level of interpersonal
relations where they dealt or failed to deal with anger and hurt and
love and hate.

After spending fourteen and seventeen hours a day together for a number of months, it was easy to see how some, crowded in their inadequate houses with three and four generations, feel trapped, as indeed they are. "I need," said Bernie, "my bottle of happiness."

They even felt themselves growing security-minded—conscious of public attention and opinion. In the beginning the possibility of failure gave them a boldness they began to lose when newspaper articles were written about them and grants came through and there was money on hand. With a few stakes out they became less and less willing to face the threat of trying things that might go wrong, and when they did take the risk and things did go wrong, they were upset.

Another difficult area was the discipline of being punctual. Their lives were full of unexpected situations which seemed to justify their not arriving on schedule. Another complication was transportation, which grew more unreliable with the passage of time. At one point David described it this way, "We had to put one of our cars permanently to pasture; the second one, which we have felt from time to time was probably found there, has been without a right rear fender for the last three weeks; the third one is without a muffler and really should be driven only in the pasture, and our blue bus is no more reliable than most early World War II buses."

Life in community was different from what they had imagined, and each was reluctant to give up his separate image of what it should be. They had done what Bonhoeffer had warned against: they had injected into the community their own human wish dreams, and this had made them accusers of each other.

They had tried to live under a common Rule and failed again and again. Even when they succeeded according to the letter, according to the spirit they did not. It was easy to be legalistic regarding another's failure and to forget the elementary fact that the Rule had no value in itself, but was to help them become available to each other and to others.

The law had done what Paul had said it would. It taught them what sin is, and it taught them a need for grace and compassion. They made changes in the Rule, but its intent remained the same. They were able to resist the temptation to modify it, reminding each other that their struggle with discipline and responsibility was part of their struggle for wholeness and freedom.

It was not only in their relationships with each other that they found some of their illusions being shattered, but in their relationships with their neighbors. They had thought of themselves as tolerant young liberals who could mediate acceptance, but instead they were often shocked by what they saw. The most disturbing sight was probably a house where many children lived. The younger children, and even an occasional mother, would urinate on the back porch or in the littered dirt alley where the children played. Said Lynn, "The flies, and smells and garbage and rats, were an aching kind of thing that can't be explained." Equally unexplainable were the children whose playground was that alley. The Covenant Community often found that their own lagging spirits were revived by the reverberating life of these children.

The older children sometimes taught the younger children to fight. It was not uncommon for them to choose two five-year-olds to pit against each other in what seemed so much like a cockfight. Lynn and Margy would watch in horror, helpless to do anything, knowing it would not be over until one of the children went down.

But if some of their play was peculiar to the street and streets like it, some was much like the play of children everywhere. "I remember," said Margy, "Rosena and Bonita and another child walking around under a tattered umbrella looking comical because they were so tattered themselves, but having a great time."

And then there was small John, who put a cardboard packing case on the stairs and had himself a slide going. And Pat, who made shoes out of smashed beer cans. With her feet in the dents she clopped around like any other little girl parading in her mother's high-heeled shoes.

They grew so close to the children of the street that they could be in the house and hear a child cry outside, and know which one it was. "It was kind of exciting," said Lynn, "like being able to tell footsteps."

They found out that it was important that they lived on the block and knew the children within that context. It helped them to know the why's of their behavior in the classroom. Slowly they became less anxious about results and what would come of all their efforts. Their attitude at first had been that of middle-class poverty planners who chart their programs to improve the future of the present-oriented poor, whose needs are too immediate for them to look to some distant reward. As Margy and Lynn became more intimately involved in their lives, they began also to think in terms of the present.

To the preschool was added an athletic program and activities for older children. One afternoon an ambulance siren interrupted a dance they were having in the basement of the Covenant Community house. The children were gone in a flash to follow it to the end of the block, where there had been a stabbing. When the ambulance had carried away the victim, the children returned—not to dance, but to imitate the stabbing for Margy and Lynn and for each other's amusement. Margy and Lynn instinctively turned away from their laughter, and then wondered if it wasn't the children's way of not letting life get too close, for events like this would be the scenes of their childhood.

During the year the community lived on Seaton Place two policemen on their beat stopped in at the Potter's House Gift Shop and fell into conversation with Mary Hitchcock about soaring crime in the District of Columbia. Not knowing that the gift shop had any relation to the Covenant Community, they began to give her an account of the "crazy young people" who had moved to Seaton Place. "We told them to stay out," said one, "but they are still there, and it's a changed block. We used to get several calls a night from that block. Now it's more like twice a month."

This was the same confirmation that Walter got when he took the children to visit the local Precinct. A policeman pointed out their street on the map. "I'm not going to tell you about Seaton Place," he said, "it's been terrible, but it's getting better."

The Covenant Community knew that their part in all of this was small. There were many agents of change on the block. There were moments too when the community was profoundly aware that there was more at work than they or anyone else could take credit for. This awareness of "something other" came most often when they were with the children, and usually in events that were not in themselves dramatic. There was the time when Walter and little Carol Lee Cruz sat and talked for an hour. "We just enjoyed being with each other and talking to each other," said Walter. "Out on the street kids are so easily distracted, but after that conversation, she would wait for me. We had shared something. We never got back to that kind of sharing, but it was in the memory of each of us—part of our relationship with each other."

There was another time very much like this for Walter. He was taking a class at the church in Christian growth, and the assignment for the week was to get to know three people better: a person well liked, a person hardly known, and a person disliked.

Walter chose Eddie for the person he did not like. Eddie was a runny-nosed five-year-old with a shrill voice and fingers that were always sticky. In the classroom his behavior was destructive. He could never stay with a task, and aimlessly followed anyone who wandered by. "We went for a walk," said Walter, "and as we walked a calm came to us both. He was not a calm child, but somehow space came into his life. We played ball in the park, and then we ambled over to the classroom so I could pick up some papers. There he began to work on something. He worked consistently and attentively for an hour with a great deal of concentration, and I watched in wonder this little boy who had seldom been still. We kind of dwelt together in our enjoyment of what he was doing and making."

These were peak experiences—a lot of life was lived short of them, and a lot of life was lived at crisis points. The Spanish write of Americans that we live our lives on a straight line—a plateau instead of from valley to peak, knowing height and depth; but this is not so of the poor. They are not so insulated from physical experience, and they do not make their plans to cover tomorrow.

One night there came an urgent pounding at their door, and David opened it to a woman who informed him that her friend across the street was about to have a baby. David went to get the truck for which they had traded a car, but when the woman came out on the street and looked at the height of the seat, she said that she could never make it up there. At that moment Walter arrived in his car, and also, much to their relief, the emergency squad which someone had called. They explained to the policeman that Walter's car had a broken gear shift and was not dependable transportation. The policeman responded that this was no emergency and that the woman could call an ambulance. David explained that she could not pay for an ambulance, but the squad departed nonetheless. With this the woman and her mother got into Walter's car and left for the hospital with David driving and Walter calling after him, "Be careful of the gear shift!" David heeded the warning, but when they arrived at an intersection he shifted gears and the car stopped. This left him nothing to do but wave wildly at passing cars. Finally one stopped and the pregnant woman, her mother, David, and a policeman whose attention they had attracted, all piled in. This policeman was so shaken up by what he concluded was an emergency that after they had passed safely through each intersection he would lean out the window and blow heartily on his whistle. Five minutes after they arrived at the hospital, the baby was born.

"I began to understand," said Walter, "what Paul Goodman admires in the poor. They don't let you be phony with them. They live closer to reality—to death and life and despair and hope. The poor have less to hide behind. There is no cushion of money and things to help them appear to themselves and to others what they are not, and they don't have people holding them to acceptable patterns of behavior."

While living with the poor deepened the group's sensitivity for basic things, it did not lessen their appreciation of the middle-class way of life. There were distortions in that life, but it also had simple pleasures that they wanted for their friends on Seaton Place. Once they visited a friend in the suburbs and found it fantastic just to lie on the grass in the evening and look up at the stars. They took pleasure in ordinary things like a table set with linen napkins and a firm bed with pressed sheets.

They had not observed when they first moved to Seaton Place that one end of the block was different from the other. It was only after they had been there for a number of months that they began to know that they were located on the "poor half" of the block, which was also the half with the concentration of small children. These were the families they got to know best. Some of those at the other end had steady employment and tried to maintain their houses. There were even some who chose to keep distance between themselves and their poorer neighbors.

More than the difference between the ends of the block, however, they came to know the differences between families. No family was like the next. They had always agreed with this in theory, but when it came to talking about the people of Seaton Place they had sometimes lumped them together as "them" or "the poor," obscuring the great individuality of life behind those words. They could no longer do this, and each of them according to their own individuality felt drawn to a different family. For David it was the Kingstons, whose house was a house of woe. He made their acquaintance first through Andrew, who was always in good humor but rarely sober. He would greet David on the street, "I want you to step into my office." He would then back up five steps and motion David in. The purpose of his request was to ask for booze. David never had any hopes of getting Andrew a job, but for Emma, Andrew's sister, he tried again and again. One day he went cheerfully to their house to tell Emma that he had a job for her. He gave the message to the man who opened the door. He was stunned when the answer was, "Emma don't need no job. Andrew is dead."

No one in the house knew why Andrew had died. Someone thought it was because he had eaten a catfish, and a child pointed excitedly to a pail with fish swimming in it. Emma asked David if he would read the obituary at the funeral. It was an elaborate statement of Andrew's march into heaven. When she found out, two hours before the funeral, that the man in New York whom she had asked to preach could not come, she told David that he would also preach the sermon.

When David pondered on what he might say at his first funeral service, he was troubled. Andrew had never held a job for any length of time. He had been dishonorably discharged from the army. He had spent his share of time in jail. He was usually drunk, and now at thirty-four he was dead of some unknown cause. This was the official record, but on the street Andrew's life had mattered, and he would be missed. He was the one in his house who on cold mornings, for the sake of the children, got up to start the stove. He had talked to David about helping Martha and Nicky in their schoolwork. He had even asked him to get help for Penny, who was retarded and had difficulty in speaking. He did not believe that his future could be different, but he believed in something new for which the children could be saved.

In the early days, when the painting on their house had gone slowly it was Andrew who had helped them paint. And then when they were still strangers and uncertain of their reception, he had introduced them to his friends. But more than this, through Andrew's life David had moved closer to finding his own identity and to knowing that at the heart of it was reconciliation—reconciliation between the conflicting forces within, and between himself and others, and between himself and Andrew. He did not hold less strongly that the battles for the poor would have to be waged in the area of housing and jobs and on the political front, but he had learned that the deeper problem is the one of reconciliation between individuals of two different races and between the individual man of affluence and the individual man of poverty. Here white and black and rich and poor would wage the major battle. He knew that if this reconciliation was to happen in his own life, he had to give up thinking of himself as belonging to the group that was rich, and white, and on top, serving a good cause.

He had understood this intellectually but it had not cut deeply into him, so that he was aware of fighting with an image of himself as the "nice guy helping out." He couldn't get rid of it. It would take him by surprise at unlikely moments. And then one day he began to see all this more clearly, and the agent of the change was Andrew. He was walking down the street with Andrew, who had just been in a fight and was battered and beat up and drunk, and as he walked beside Andrew he became aware that involved in their reconciliation was his own acceptance of what he and his people had been and had done to this man. Deep in him there flashed that what he and Andrew both shared in common was the need for forgiveness.

Remembering this, David knew that the funeral service was not a time for him to try to justify Andrew's life. Of all that he would say, perhaps the most important was that "we are here to offer thanks to God that all of us in some way or another have shared in the gift of Andrew's life."

Spring came, and the seventh child was born to Doris and Ray Cheeks. They had no name for him and Margy said, "Call him Thaddeus Jeffrey," and they called him Thaddeus Jeffrey.

Also, in the spring they got Rudy's saxophone out of hock.

And in the spring came word from the Washington Office of Operation Headstart that their request for $5,850 to operate a Headstart center had been granted, which meant that the preschool could continue through the summer with an additional teacher and classroom.

Also in the spring, the United Planning Organization promised them a grant of $6,000 to operate a Summer Neighborhood Activities Program (SNAP) for children between the ages of six and twelve. Some of their advisers wanted it held at the Potomac School in Virginia, where the children would have the woods to run in. Others suggested the neighborhood, so that they could learn to live creatively on their own streets. The Covenant Community decided for the streets and rented space in a garage for a woodshop and in a basement for a sewing center. They later secured the basement of a vacant house for a music and drama center, and a large room in a neighborhood church for an art program. One day a week they went to the Potomac School for that run in the woods. Another day each week a Washington merchant living in Virginia let them use his swimming pool.

One hundred children were enrolled in the program. The staff included fifteen "well-paid" teen-agers from the neighborhood and fifteen "not so well-paid" teen-agers from the suburbs. Despite the differences of background, they acted as a unit with that charismatic power that comes to a group which is committed to something beyond itself. As with many small groups working with poverty funds, money was a problem. In this instance the money that was promised in June did not come for fifteen more months, and then it was $2,000 less than they had been promised.

Through the summertime the Covenant Community house was more full of small children than in the days when the preschool met there. They were always at the door begging entrance, eager for conversation or simply wanting to come in and observe. When a group of children had been there, the house would have to be searched after they left to be certain all had departed, or an hour later they would hear a giggle or see a little face peering up behind the sofa or around a chair.

Probably best of all, the children loved to watch Margy and

Lynn cook dinner. The simple combinations of food fascinated them. "You going to cook that? What are you putting in there? Can I have some?" The fact of a table being set each night and each of their tall friends having a place to sit was a ritual foreign to them and a never-ending source of fascination. Many of these children were handed something to eat when they appeared in their own kitchens, and would eat standing up, or sitting on their doorsteps.

On Seaton Place life always seemed close to the group. It was never at a distance. They felt it especially in the summer when so much of it was lived on the street. The people would play cards on the sidewalk, or have dances in the street, or just sit on the steps visiting with each other. Somehow they would fill the street all through the day and evening with an unbelievable amount of noise. Once at the school, when David came upon little Ricky standing thoughtfully before a picture of Christ walking on a path through the woods, he asked the boy what he was thinking, and Ricky replied, "I would like to walk like that where there is quiet."

Through the summer months they were often tired and sometimes overwhelmed by the complexity of life on the street and life in their own house. Gordon stopped by one day, and after listening for a while to their troubles asked them whether they would choose to be some other place if they could. They answered a strong No, but Margy added, "We had no idea what we were getting into." He laughed at that and said, "The most helpful experiments are accomplished by people who are too naïve to know what they are getting into. The wise and experienced know too much ever to accomplish the impossible."

Another visitor asked them a different kind of question. "Do you give more to the street or does the street give more to you?" David probably answered for them all when he said, "I guess you give what you can give, and hope you are open to receive. We have youth and can teach. They have age and experience. Possibly, though, the only times any of us give are those times when we share together our uncertainties and anxieties—when we are willing to explore life together. I think the question is not who has the most to give, but are we freer to participate more fully in life because of what has happened between us, freer to be honest, to give up some of the illusions we have? I think the answer is probably Yes."

The summer SNAP program came to an end with a street carnival and, of course, a parade. At the head of the parade was Rudy playing on his saxophone.

The churches—now four, including Bishop Reed's—formed with the parents an official board to administer the preschool program and to assure its continuation in the next years. And members of the Covenant Community wrestled with the decision of whether to stay on Seaton Place another year. Jim planned to marry, but to continue his work on the street as president of the Community Council. Lynn decided to teach in the preschool, but not to live in the community. Margy took a job with the Advanced Linguistic Center and was assigned to work on Seaton Place in a program to study the speech problems and patterns of deprived children. David decided to return to Union Seminary and finish his B.D. Only Walter chose to stay on in the Covenant House. Part of the sadness and the guilt that touched them in making their decisions was the knowledge that they were free to choose, and were leaving behind friends to whom choices were not offered. They had learned that to be poor is to have few choices.

When David came to his decision he went to tell Grandmother Kingston, the oldest woman on the block and the grandmother of Andrew. She was the golden person to say his name. "David," she said, "I don't want to see you go, but you have to finish studying to be a preacher, because you preached good over Andrew."

In this way the first year of the Covenant Community came to an end. Each knew that they had not accomplished what they had dreamed about when they had planned a community "that would exist to build itself in Christ." And yet, this had happened in ways different from what they had imagined. In their relationships with one another they had found in themselves areas of need and had become aware of problems that were still unresolved. The long days they had spent together gave them to know that in them dwelt sin, and that this is what all men have in common. The darkness they found in the street was the same darkness they found in their own hearts. This seemed the most important thing that had happened to them—perhaps as important as the love which was between them and bore witness to the healing presence of Christ.

If anyone at the year's end had asked them to define the Community, they would have pushed aside elaborate definitions and said simply that it was the attempt of a few people to struggle with who they were and what they might be. It seemed also to them that there were those on Seaton Place engaged in that same struggle.

10

For Love of Children

God is Lord of history. He speaks in events. He does not choose the mighty, but the weak. He does not choose Rome, but Bethlehem—not a throne, but a cradle—not a crown, but a cross. In March, 1965, He was not different, He still looked to the lowly. He addressed the churches of America through an unlikely town and an unlikely people. He did not choose Washington, D.C., but Selma, Alabama; not the country club there, but a Negro church in a remote section of town; not the astronauts who were circling the earth, but a little band of people who traveled on foot the fifty miles along U.S. Highway 80 between Selma and Montgomery. And across the country, churches which could not find life in the symbols they had, found a new and living one in that line of marchers. It might die as other symbols die, but for a time, which may still endure, it had the power of every living symbol, to transform, and change, and heal.

The events out of which it came went back a hundred years, but they did not crash in on our community until that night of March

6 when we watched on television sets the brutal clubbing and
blocking of demonstrators in Selma as they began a march to
Montgomery. In Washington, D.C. we have no vote, because we
have no home rule, and whereas this is the cause of much distress
in this city, it had never occurred to any of us that we might march
for the right to vote. After Selma, we thought of it, along with
other things that needed doing. But that was later.

Now our neighbors were being kicked and clubbed in Alabama,
and we had so long done nothing that when moved to act, there
was nothing we knew to do. The next morning we just went to
work as usual. Most of us even missed hearing that the Rev. Dr.
Martin Luther King had issued a call to the clergymen of America
to join him in Selma for a second march. Others more alert did
hear and swung into action to issue the call again, now on a local
level. It was 3:30 P.M. when Paul Carr finally reached Gordon to
tell him that the Council of Churches of Greater Washington had
chartered a plane for the clergy who would leave National Airport at 4:30 P.M. Gordon left for Selma, along with forty other
ministers. Those of us who knew he had gone called the members
of the church to alert them to pray. We found out that it is one
thing to pray for marchers, and another thing to pray for marchers
when your leader is among them. The next day we worked by our
radios, and gathered at night in our homes to watch on television
the events in Selma.

When Gordon returned, he described in his Sunday sermon
some of the scenes that he and hundreds of others would
never forget. The night the group of ministers from Washington
arrived in Selma, they had gone to the Brown's Chapel, where a
mass meeting was held in preparation for the new march. His was
the first contingent to arrive of what was to be wave after wave of
white clergymen from all over the nation. Every aisle and balcony
was filled, and hundreds of people were standing outside when an
elderly woman began the song that all joined in singing,

> Mine eyes have seen the glory
>   of the coming of the Lord.
> He is trampling out the vintage
>   Where the grapes of wrath are stored.

"I've never heard it sung that way in my life," said Gordon, "and in that moment I knew it was right that we were there. You could see the hope written on the faces lined with suffering, and the message, 'Tomorrow we shall not walk alone.' " Later that night, the man in whose home Gordon was staying said, "I watched you coming in. It was the most beautiful sight I've ever seen in my life when you walked in. I'd have almost given up my place in glory to have seen that sight."

In the crowded quarters of his Negro host, the rising hour was 5:00 A.M. "In that little space of time between five and six-thirty," said Gordon, "I saw as beautiful a piece of family life as I've ever watched. It was characterized by the respect of the parents for each other and for the children, and the respect of the children for the parents, and the teamwork of all. The eleven-year-old prepared lunches for all five children and his mother, and then fixed everyone a breakfast of scrambled eggs and hominy grits. During that time the mother braided the hair of each little girl. It took fifteen minutes for each pair of braids and she had three to do. There was only one crisis in the family. Little five-year-old Louise with her spindly legs wanted to go on the march, and they wouldn't let her. "You can criticize the parents," said Gordon, "for letting the children be in the forefront of the movement, but the problem is you can't keep them out."

There was the morning rally at the church, where they were taught nonviolent ways of protecting themselves. One of the clergymen asked, "If they are beating us, may we grab the billy stick?" The sixteen-year-old who was briefing the group of bishops and other clergy said, "Absolutely no. This is exactly what they are waiting for, and if you are unable to keep from grabbing the billy stick, don't you go on this march."

Then came the charge to the adults by this same teen-age veteran. "Everyone knows," he said, "that the students are the backbone of this movement, but the backbone is not much good without flesh. You adults are the flesh. Today when we are on this march I want you adults to behave like adults. The children and even the teen-agers panic first. But you have lived longer than the rest of us and you ought to know how to deport yourselves. You act like adults this afternoon because we need you."

Then there was the appearance of the Rev. Martin Luther King —a young Moses ready to lead his people. For him Pharaoh had said No, and God had said Yes.

There was the march itself, back over that same course the marchers had trudged the day before—across the ground where the tear gas had been thrown, and some in the crowd had panicked, and police horses had trampled helpless victims, and the troopers and posse had beaten women, children, and men. "I had the feeling," said Gordon, "that I was going intentionally into a trap, watching the exits close and knowing there was no way of getting free. You couldn't get out to the east or the west or the north or the south. They could beat you back up this path with every exit closed. The feeling I'd never known before was that in the springing of the trap there was nothing you could do. We could not fight our way out. We were committed to doing nothing rather than violate the witness."

What Gordon said that Sunday morning was that to be in Selma was to touch a spirit and go away changed. "What I saw there was a people being wounded for our transgressions, who were being bruised for our iniquities.* When there is need," he added, "we shall go to where the battleground is, but the real battleground for most of us is Washington and the acute need that is here."

In those days after the march newscasters and reporters wondered what life would be like for the Selma Negroes when the bishops and the nuns and the young men with beards and crewcuts and hound's-tooth jackets, and the more tattered army of freedom workers were gone—not to mention the army of reporters and television cameras. As the army of FLOC (For Love of Children) grows and conquers and marches and sings, we have often thought back to Selma and wondered also. In the high moments of FLOC we think. "Tell its story on the mountain," and then we remember those days in the spring of 1965 and think, "No, tell its story on Sylvan Street in Selma."

For those who had been there, Selma became the symbol for every community in our nation. If Selma had its mansions and its shacks—poverty and affluence side by side—so did New York, Cleveland, Chicago, Los Angeles, and Washington. In Washington

* See Isa. 53.

we do not even keep our poverty hidden away as many cities do. Our squalor encroaches on embassy row. The front door of The Potter's House opens on a modest but thriving street; its back door on one of the slum areas of the city. It has been here for a long time, and if you had asked us if we saw it, we would have said, "Yes, we see it. Haven't we told you about the Covenant Community, and there are other things besides"—and there would have been those other things to name. But after Selma it was different. It was the miracle of being able to say, "Once we were blind and now we see."

While other groups focused on home rule, integrated housing, and education, our own attention turned to Junior Village, the District's dismal institution for homeless children. For years the newspapers had run editorials and feature articles which described the plight of these children in an overcrowded, understaffed institution. One reporter wrote, "They are being crippled as surely as if you heard their bones cracking." Some of us knew firsthand, because we had worked there as volunteers for a twelve-month period. We had begun in the cottage for four-year-olds and had chosen the bedtime hours because they were the hours when there would be need for stories, extra kisses, fluffed pillows—that host of little attentions one gives so naturally to children at the end of a day.

Any idyllic pictures we had of the magical hour of bedtime were shattered the first night, when we were assigned our posts in the bathtub assembly line. To give any child more than the time needed to wash him was to place an extra burden on the line of his waiting companions. Still, we were aware that for the child in the tub those few moments were the only ones in the day when he would have the sole attention of an adult and know the touch of human hands. Occasionally, a child managed the feat of smuggling into the line a second time. We struggled to forget that forty children were to be bathed in an hour, and tried to give to every child the gift of seeing him, but often despaired, because wedging its way in was the thought, "What can it matter against all the anonymous minutes of his day?"

Finally, all forty would be in their pajamas and in the dormitory room with its narrow double-decked beds. In our early innocence we would sometimes kneel to hug one, and every starving child standing by would scream to be held. Through the uproar the attendant asked us please not to show special attention to any child, or none of them would settle down for the night. On order, they climbed obediently into their beds, some of them sleeping two in a bed. As we passed through the room little arms would reach out and little voices call softly, "Mama, mama, mama—" When the lights went off, a room of forty four-year-olds was filled with a swift silence that the mother of even one four-year-old would know as unnatural, and we crept down the corridors defeated— glad to have for another week the bedtime hour of children in Junior Village behind us.

After a number of months with the four-year-olds, we asked to be transferred to the cottage for babies. It had occurred to us that we might be able to do more for the babies. Again we had con- jured up a false picture—this time of sweet-smelling, cuddly babies that we would rock and play with for an hour. Instead, they were wet, foul-smelling, with vacant eyes. A room of babies, and seldom did you hear one cry. Unlike the older children, they did not respond to words or touch, but lay listless in their cribs. Even in our wild imagining, it had never seemed possible to be a baby and not be held, but the cribs were there—row on row bearing mute testimony to that terrible fact.

In March of 1965 the population of Junior Village had almost reached its all-time high and was hovering around 910 children. The younger the child, the more damaging is institutional life, and most of the children at Junior Village were not yet six. The cottage which had been built for the toddlers and was meant to have 8 to a room had 12 and 13—sometimes 16. The one nurse provided to take care of the eight also had to care for every additional child that was herded in.

It would be easy to say that Junior Village was the failure of Washington's welfare system, but what we began to understand was that we had no claim to innocence. Washington was not Nazi Germany, where to act would cost one's life. We could cease to wonder how the people of that unhappy land had silently watched so much death. For a decade, without audible protest, we had allowed the nation's capital to dump its helpless children into seven old buildings, which a half-century ago had been erected as a reformatory for Negro boys, and now were firetraps that should be torn down. Long before the spring of 1965, the number of children per staff worker had reached a criminal imbalance. But it was not better-staffed, newer, larger, finer buildings that the children of Junior Village needed. They needed homes—not an institution. The few modern buildings there could be saved for a children's psychiatric treatment center in a city that had none.

A home for every child in Junior Village before a year was over was the mission that was shaping in our minds and hearts. In his second sermon following the Selma march, Gordon issued to the whole congregation the call to join the mission to free the children of Junior Village. The requisites for participation were more stringent and carefully defined than they had been for other missions. The practical-minded and logical were warned that this might not be a mission for which they were temperamentally suited. There would be no committees to reason and argue endlessly whether this could be done and cautiously experiment here and there. We had already accepted the opinion of the experts that it was impossible. This was a mission to do the impossible. Not only that, but to be in this mission one had to hear the call to do the impossible as good news—no long faces in this mission. The debonair spirit of the freedom movement was to mark it.

"If you do not find me in the march, look for me over in the graveyard, for that's where I'll be." This spirit and commitment unto death were the requisites for joining. "We so carefully watch," said Gordon, "the limits of our health and strength, for some of us are very tired. We measure out the love that we give to others as from a medicine dropper. But under the baptism of the Spirit, I have seen limits disappear. People walk who can't walk— the too old, the too young, the too responsible, are all at it in the most irresponsible and refreshing way. I am deeply sympathetic with the limits—I understand them, but the power of the Spirit when the limits disappear is heady stuff."

Gordon was careful to explain that the earlier calls we had heard were still valid in most cases, that not everyone was called to participate in this particular need. "Sometimes," he said, "we think that if we are not at the growing edge of the church and doing what

currently concerns its energy and interest, we are not in the main-
stream of life." He emphasized that this was not true and that
those previous calls were the wide, diverse base which enabled us
seriously to consider this new call. He used as an example the
retreat mission. "Unless that mission can help us get our roots
down into the life of God, the springs for this or any other mission
will not flow."

Thirty persons responded to the call—the largest number that
had responded to any mission call up to that time. The strategy the
members decided on was to contact some fifteen hundred churches
in the Washington area and issue to them the call that Gordon had
issued to us. The thought was that if a hundred of these churches
would each form a mission group, each group could concentrate
on finding homes for ten children, and in a year the job would be
done.

The mission called itself FLOC, For Love of Children. In its
early meetings, strategy was planned and duties assigned. The primary tasks were to assemble every relevant detail into so-called
fact kits and send out teams of two to visit the ministers of Washington churches. The teams were briefed on the facts of the mission,
but also reminded that "proclamation" means sharing what God is
doing in our midst. It is never exhortation. Any ministers who
indicated interest were invited to a luncheon where they received
the newly compiled fact kit and were invited to join the crusade
and start mission groups in their own churches.

In the fact kit, which was to be the first in a series, was a short
history of Junior Village:

    1948—opened with 90 children
    1949—population 150
    1958—population 303
    1964—population 850
    1965—population 902

The records of 340 children who had recently been admitted to
Junior Village revealed that 79 were there because their fathers
were unemployed and their families in extreme want. In the case of
74 other children, the cause was the inability of their families to
pay their rent. The most frequent cause was eviction. Among the

children sent to Junior Village as a result of eviction, one third were the victims of housing and health code enforcement. Most of these children had been living in inadequate quarters with relatives. When housing officials ordered them to leave, there was no place for them but Junior Village. Other children were from families who had been living in condemned buildings and could find nothing else because of Washington's severe housing shortage for Negro families. Others were evicted by landlords who planned to renovate to meet District requirements, but also to raise the rent. Junior Village represented in microcosm the sum total of the city's sore spots in housing, employment, discrimination, disenfranchisement, and welfare legislation. The relationship between these critical issues and the swelling population of Junior Village was evident. The focal points of action for the new mission were clear.

From the fifteen hundred churches contacted, about a hundred ministers came to the briefing sessions or sent interested laymen. Of these, only a handful were to make any firm commitment to the mission. At first glance, the effort might have seemed a failure, but what we have discovered is that our idea of how things ought to be accomplished is not always the way it is going to happen. We are coming to believe with Gamaliel that if a movement is only of our own human willing, it will collapse, but if it is of God, nothing will stop it (Acts 5:38-39). We weren't given a great army of ministers, but we were given the handful that were needed at that particular moment. Out of those who signed up as core members, the executive ecumenical council was elected. They were Jack Manley of Fairfax Baptist Church, Randy Taylor of the Church of the Pilgrims (Presbyterian), Edward McGowan of Mt. Zion Methodist Church, and Gordon Cosby of our own fellowship. Later a fifth member was added, Frederic S. Lawrence of the National Advent Christian Church. The Lord spoke to Fred directly without any assistance on our part. In the early days of FLOC he appeared at the Church of the Saviour to say that he was ready to help wherever he was needed. We told him that those were dangerous words around here and he said that he didn't care. He had thrown caution to the wind and wanted to be involved in the work of the city wherever God might choose. So we told him about FLOC, and he coordinated for us the first program to let the city of Washington know that FLOC existed. It was an art show.

After exploring ways in which we could communicate to the heart and conscience of Washington the plight of Junior Village children, we decided to let the children do it themselves through their own paintings. As had happened so many times before, the other missions of the church were needed to launch this new one. We asked The Potter's House Workshop, whose call is in the field of arts, to work with the children to express themselves in this medium. Not only did the Workshop respond with enthusiasm, but Kay Pitchford, the director, who is also an art professor at Howard University, said that she would ask her students to work with the children. The Potter's House designated six weeks when the work of the new young artists could hang on its walls, which are used to display the work of promising painters.

One Saturday, a day chosen by Junior Village officials, twenty members of the Workshop and students of Howard University arrived at Junior Village laden with oils and paints and crayons and paper. Within themselves, they carried that necessary ingredient for calling forth gifts: the expectation that they could give these children an experience in art. They worked for four hours—two in the morning and two in the afternoon—and in that time met 220 children ranging in age from four to sixteen.

Yolande Ford, a member of both FLOC and the Workshop group, was stationed with several students in a supply room to give out materials as they were needed. The children were divided among four classrooms, and it was arranged that whenever an instructor ran out of supplies, he could send a child to get more. Yolande soon discovered that she was at the nerve center where the conversations of the children coming in and out put her in touch with what was happening in each of the rooms, and more than that, with what was happening in Junior Village. The most frequent visitor was a little girl who would stop to talk to them as she passed through their room to the adjacent washroom. The first time, her hands were yellow and they laughed and joked about that; and then she washed them. The second time, her hands were black, and they laughed and hugged her over that; then she had green hands, and then brown. Finally, they perceived that she had painted her hands in order to have the physical contact of the hugs and the laughter. As long as they were there, she returned again and again with a different color on her hands.

Another group came to the supply room, among whom was a little girl who discovered that her name was the same as one of the Howard students. Every child in the group automatically gave her to the student:

"Is that your mother?"

"No."

"Why couldn't it be your mother?"

"It might be your mother."

"How do you know it isn't your mother?"

"Where is your sister? Run, get your sister. Tell her to come see someone who might be your mother."

The little group stayed with Yolande and the students in the supply room. They had many conversations. One went something like this.

"Did you know me when I was little?"

"No, not when you were little, but I have been here before and it might be that I have seen you."

"I wonder. I ask everyone because I wonder sometimes what it was like so I always ask. No one has ever told me, but I always wonder what it was like to be little."

In the classrooms the teachers were also finding out something about life at Junior Village. The drawings had the same childlike quality present in the drawings of children everywhere, whether from happy or unhappy homes. But in the drawings of Junior Village children there was also darkness. This was especially true in the work of the youngest ones. They had not lived long enough to build a wall and hide themselves behind it. Even their self-portraits had their message. One upset little girl interlaced with hundreds of lines her portrait of herself, revealing her distorted image of who she was.

One child greeted his teacher with the simple statement, "I hate you. I hate everybody. I only like my mother and father." Most of the children met them with noisy exuberance, except for one little boy who walked to his seat and proceeded to take off his shoes and stockings. Kay said, "I guess we can all remember a time when we did this, but there was something different about this child, and pretty soon we gathered that what he was saying to us was, 'I am one in a class, one in a number, and I want to be known just as I am, and if I can't have attention that way I will have it by doing what the others are not doing.' " They ran the gamut of entreating, pleading, and petting, and finally with firmness placed the shoes back on his feet and lifted him into his own seat. A few minutes later he was engrossed in painting, and when he left he touched the arm of his teacher and with a delightful childish grin said, "I was good, and I did good work, didn't I?"

The work of the older children also showed darkness. Representative of many pictures was a drawing with small figures that had hollow eyes and ghostlike heads, long attentuated bodies and no arms. This isolated group with its message of aloneness was one child's concept of the happy class that had gathered to do its creative work.

Now and then a painting expressed gayety and hope. The wonder was not that these notes were so often missing, but that they existed at all.

A high spot in the day for Yolande and Lydia Mosher was in the afternoon when they worked with the teen-agers, who immediately became engrossed in painting. "We have never had," said Yolande, "a more meaningful statement of appreciation than that of the counselor who said 'I have never before seen them keep their thoughts away from what haunts them more than five minutes at a time.' " They had been working consistently for an hour and a half. "They found out," said Yolande, "that it was possible to reflect a personality on a piece of paper with paint, crayon, and chalk." It was possible to know that one was different from one's neighbor. With blank papers in front of them, they each had set out to do the same thing and automatically had done it in different ways. It was a revelation. They were seeing themselves as someone other than one of the girls in Cottage B. In the space of a few hours they were discovering that they were owners of totally different personalities. "I had been an art teacher for years," said Yolande, "but I had never seen children making that discovery in such a vivid way."

A little boy's crying marred the closing minutes for Lydia. In the room where she had been working the counselor had lined the children up, and at the head of the line was a child who suddenly burst into tears. In her concern Lydia put out a hand to him, but the counselor said, "No, no, pay that no attention. He does that all the time. No one knows why, and we really haven't the time to stop and find out."

It was true. There was no time to find out. The task was to get the children from "here to there" before the bell sounded, and so there was the drawing of a clock face by the child asked to draw his own portrait. "Who am I? I am the one who gets up at seven o'clock. I am the one who eats at one o'clock. I am the one who naps at two o'clock. You are the one who comes at four o'clock. Who am I? It is impossible to know."

When the class of Howard students left, they knew that once was not enough. They would go back on a regular basis.

In the custom of The Potter's House, a reception was held for the young artists on the Monday before the exhibit opened to the public. Sixty-five excited boys and girls walked through the doors. Less restrained than other artists, they ran to the walls in search of their pictures, grabbing the hands of Workshop members they recognized and pointing out, "This is mine! That's mine!" And then something happened. There was a conversation overheard. Because we were not allowed to identify the Junior Village children, their pictures did not have names on them, but underneath some we had copied lines of poetry that helped to tell their story. Under one quotation from an unknown author, there was the single word "unknown." A little boy paused before the picture and said to another child,

"That's my picture!"

The other little boy said,

"Oh, no, it isn't. Look under here. There's the word 'unknown.' "

There was a split-second silence and then the childlike voice replying,

"But I am unknown."

Yolande was standing by the punch bowl when a teen-age girl with whom she had worked came up and squeezed her arm.

Yolande greeted her and they exchanged embraces, but still the child clung to her. Then she finally said in the whisper she always spoke in,

"Do you remember Ella Sanders?"

"Yes," said Yolande, "I remember her—a tall girl."

"Yes. She has been released."

Then she added,

"Do you remember Harriette? She sat in the last aisle, next to me."

"Yes, I remember."

In this way she went through four names and each time she said,

"She has been released." It was her way of saying to Yolande, "Help me with the fact that I have not been released."

To the several hundred people who came to the opening of the show, Yolande said, "We have hung these pictures because we want to release those who have not been released. It is the most graphic way we have of letting you know about a need so desperate that there is no adequate way to convey the depth and intensity of it."

On the post inside the doors of The Potter's House was printed in large letters the statement,

> Who can describe the world as it is seen through the eyes of a lost and homeless child? No words convey his strange anxiety and paralyzing fears, his cautious delight, his loss of hope, his hunger for love, or his concepts of identity and relationships, his feeling of insecurity and hurt and all his felt need. Line, form and colors have been the mute language in which he would share his inner self with us. Look with discernment then for here is revealed a poignant message from the children of Junior Village.

In order to give our two hundred invited guests some help with interpreting the pictures, we invited Ray Minsky, who had served at Junior Village as a child development specialist, to tell us what he saw in the paintings. He told an even grimmer story than we had read there. Of the lovely picture of a tree branch with a solitary leaf suspended in air, which so many had asked to purchase, he said, "This reveals the child separated from any living object. It stands for children separated from their parents, children separated from their rights." Then he went on to say, "I see before me the drawing of a rocket and an outline drawing of the United States and I think of all the things which children usually draw, children who have the security and love of their families and whose pictures have the figures of the home—a mother and a father and a child and everyone holding hands—the personal objects with which we are all familiar. I notice that these are all conspicuously absent—a rocket, and an outline map of the United States, which is not sectioned off into hometown, U.S.A., or Washington, D.C.—just an outline map, a loss of identity. A few minutes ago I wandered around this exhibit and saw a face enmeshed in black, connoting the depression of children. I saw no animals. I saw a lot of proportional inaccuracy. I saw poor relationships of objects one to another—I could go through this list and talk about no homes with gardens, no schoolhouses with teachers and blackboards and erasers. There are instead the amorphous figurations of the child who cannot express himself, the child who has had such a limited experiential background and is so impoverished, so emotionally distraught that he cannot express his feelings in any form or symbolism that would communicate to us. Everywhere I look I see nothing which conveys to me the types of drawings I see from other children. The children of Junior Village are unique—products of homes which have been in the process of disintegration. They have been rejected.

"I can only summarize by saying that I have heard the children of Junior Village cry out in the night and I have been listening and listening for a response. Tonight I think I hear it in the echo of FLOC—For Love of Children."

Another speaker was J. W. Anderson, editorial writer for the *Washington Post,* who had for a long time been writing about Junior Village in the pages of that newspaper and recently had published an article in *Harper's Magazine,* entitled "A Special Hell for Children in Washington."

That night Mr. Anderson pointed out that the pictures on the walls of The Potter's House had been done by children five and older and were the work of the older half of the institution's population. These he told us were by and large the least vulnerable children. The younger ones—the ones too young to express themselves in this fashion—react even more sharply than these children do.

He also said that one out of every four children at Junior Village was ill every week with a virus infection as a result of overcrowding. He said that these illnesses could contribute to poor development, so that the child at Junior Village was not only psychologically hurt but could be physically damaged. He stated that it was an established fact that children separated from their parents are more vulnerable to disease. Not only do they get sick more easily, but once sick, they stay sick longer and more seriously. This might have explained the picture that was just colors except for a carefully drawn medicine cabinet in one corner with the bold letters: MEDICINES.

Mr. Anderson said that Junior Village had always been an anomaly to him. "Washington," he reminded us, "is one of the wealthiest cities that mankind has ever known. It has the highest per capita income of any city in the world, and a remarkable wealth of organizational talent and professional knowledge and skills. It seems that we could do better than we are doing for these children."

Dr. Randolph Taylor, speaking for the FLOC ecumenical council, gave some explanation when he said that Junior Village was the focus of the indifference, hostility, avoidance of pain, and anonymity which are part of every city. "If this city will wake up and see what it is doing to those whom it does not intend to injure at all, there may yet be hope for the lives and personalities reflected in these images around us. What can you do?" he asked that gathering, among whom were some of Washington's elite. "You can begin by seeing, because this institution which no one wanted and which no one planned is there because we haven't been looking."

As FLOC organized for action it concentrated on four areas: (1) foster homes, (2) legislation and social design, (3) home rehabilitation, and (4) group homes. In our own church, mission groups came into existence around each of these concerns. Earlier we had wrestled with the question of how much attention the mission groups would give to the inward journey. Could we move faster, if we sacrificed the common life of worship and study and prayer, and gave all our time and energy to the gigantic task of becoming informed and of acting? Should we leave any theological reflection to some future day when the task was done? Perhaps coffee houses had time for prayer, while missions to free children did not.

When the debate was over, it was decided once again to keep in balance the inward and the outward journey. We knew we could never learn what we would have to know to reach the goal that lay before us. In our own strength, we could never move the mountains that already loomed. There was in each of us one whose confidence was in the Lord, who listened to him and rested in the promise that, when we acted on his Word, he would equip us for our task. This was the part of us that had to be tended and helped to grow—for "our name is Legion." The enemies are within. No matter how great would be the opposing forces without, the real resistance would be found in ourselves, for there is a part of us that would retire from the battle. There is one in us that does not know the things that belong to its peace, that believes it has a right to large amounts of leisure, of comfort and the world's goods, that thinks it is injured by hard work. And there is another who whispers cautious words, who needs to know exactly how things will turn out, and that tomorrow will be better than today. Against these voices and other unknown foes we decided for those disciplines that would strengthen that one in us who is running after Christ, who believes that Junior Village is God's mission, and that it goes into a fight where Another already is.

FLOC's first project was a door-to-door canvass to find foster homes for 400 children who could be moved immediately from Junior Village, if suitable homes were found. Every Saturday for eight weeks about thirty persons from the FLOC missions gathered at Mt. Zion Church to sing FLOC songs and receive instructions on procedure. From there they went out in teams of two to work in specific areas of the city. For most of them going forth to knock on doors required a girding up of the loins. Each time it seemed unbelievable that they were going to knock on the doors of perfect strangers to ask if they would like a little child to live with them.

When the morning was over, they gathered again to share their experiences. Much to their surprise, they found that they had been invited into many homes, and that in one morning eleven applications were signed and filed with the Department of Public Welfare for processing. There was no incentive of money to prompt the signing of these applications, for while it costs $300 a month to keep a child in Junior Village, the average rate for a child in a foster home is $75 a month. Welfare pays $32 monthly to keep a child in his own home. All this was part of the Junior Village picture, and prompted them to put in a word along the way for Home Rule in the District.

When the first weeks of the canvassing were over, they had netted 174 foster home candidates, but between April and October only 30 of those applications had been processed. A personnel shortage in the Department of Welfare became evident, and long conversations began between FLOC and the Welfare officials. The rejection of so many candidates also had led FLOC workers to press for a reevaluation of the criteria for acceptable foster parents and homes.

Of the 400 children that FLOC had set out to find homes for, none had actually been placed as of November, 1965. The canvassers were not discouraged. They felt that they had become aware of new areas for action, and that the campaign had raised some of the crucial issues of Junior Village for more than five hundred persons.

In their canvass of the churches, they found that there were times when a minister did respond enthusiastically, but could not stir his congregation; conversely, a layman would get excited and then be disappointed because he could not interest his minister. As the anticipated number of small mission groups in other churches failed to form, it became evident that the organizational strategy of FLOC had to change. It was being forced into even more ecumenical structures, which would enable anyone to participate without requiring a mission group in his own church. The FLOC executive board agreed to ask existing groups that had been formed within the churches to disband and form again, so that instead of there being a foster-home-finding group or a home rehabilitation group in each church, there would be one or more ecumenical groups in each of these areas, made up of members from many churches. This recommendation was presented at a meeting of 72 people attending from 16 churches in the area. The Plan was adopted and the FLOC commitment hammered through to read:

I. FLOC membership means primarily a personal commitment to God as revealed in Christ. This implies active involvement in FLOC *and* a local congregation.

II. The commitment will become specific at the point of certain disciplines:

1. Work in a FLOC group.

2. Worship in a FLOC group *and* in one's own congregation.

3. Daily prayer and devotional study.

4. Financial support of FLOC (perhaps small but regular).

5. Training to prepare for participation in mission.

6. Unqualified acceptance of other FLOC members and willingness to minister to them when needed.

7. Willingness to interpret FLOC, its nature and purpose.

It is possible for individuals to participate at one of three levels. Those who subscribe fully to the commitment and discipline are the *core members*. *Associate members* are those who participate, but are not prepared to assume the complete commitment and discipline. *Supporting members* give such support to FLOC as interest and available time allow.

As churches across the country become more mission-oriented, there are many informal discussions around the question of whether the ordained minister should not earn his living in a secular calling and participate as anyone else in the life of the church. It is easy to see that a church trying to understand what it means to strip for action should think of its excesses and unnecessary endowments, but the new shaping of the church's life to the needs of the world is going to call for, not less leadership, but a different kind of leadership. The church is going to be vastly limited in what it can do, if there are not those who can give all their waking hours to building the structures that will call forth the gifts of the laity and equip them for their ministry as pastors and teachers and healers and prophets. In the first year of FLOC, Yolande Ford, on a part-time basis, did the immense job of coordinating the FLOC activities, which enabled the mission groups to "dig in" where they could be most effective. Because of family responsibilities, she could not continue indefinitely, however, and it became obvious that FLOC needed a full-time director. The man named for that post was Fred Taylor. Fred was an ordained Baptist minister whose background fitted him uniquely for the leadership of FLOC. He had a degree from Yale Divinity School, had had pastorates for seven years, and had worked in the area of group dynamics. While still employed by the Work Training Opportunity Center in the District of Columbia, he had sat in with the planning group of FLOC and marched with the legal action group, and he and his wife and three children had knocked on doors with the Foster Home Finding Group. We had learned again that, though we may do the calling, it is God who raises up the man.

Reflecting on the new ecumenical structure of the FLOC groups, Yolande summed up a basic change in attitude by saying, "We have turned from a crusade—'Free the children immediately, Lord, immediately!'—into a mission that might involve us for the rest of our days."

Fred described it in another way, "While public officials have been confronted and the spotlight of publicity turned on the problem of Junior Village, the results of the crusade are still like the first visit of Moses and Aaron before Pharaoh when they sought the release of the children of Israel. Pharaoh didn't budge. Neither did the regulations, the apathy, the interwoven economic, social, political, and spiritual factors which make up the Pharaoh behind Junior Village. FLOC learned as did Moses and Aaron, that if we really want to set the children free, we will have to stay at it, and at it, and at it. Pharaoh has to be shown."

When FLOC shifted its emphasis from a crusade to small committed and disciplined ecumenical mission groups, the work of the groups intensified and broadened in scope. Almost every time they met, gifts were discovered, and this determined the direction in which they moved. The Foster Home recruitment program continued, along with communication with the public and church groups. Brochures were written and circulated, social and legislative research initiated. There was also FLOC's first experience in lobbying, the training of a singing chorus of "Young Voices" at Junior Village, and the beginning of classes for the orientation and training of prospective members of FLOC.

FLOC had placed an ad in local newspapers announcing that a twelve-week training course for the mission would be held at Mt. Zion Methodist Church. Sixty-five people came to see what it was all about and attended one or two sessions. Of the 25 who completed the course, 18 became the associate and core members of two new mission groups. One chose as its task the establishing of a halfway house for boys that were soon to be dismissed from Junior Village. John Schramm, minister of the Lutheran Community of Christ, was this group's moderator. Everyone in the group took responsibility for different details in the planning and implementation. A guiding spirit was Don McNaughton, who had worked at Junior Village as a scoutmaster and had always wondered about the boys who "graduated" to community life after years there. "They are seventeen or eighteen when they leave," he said, "but they are still children, who become easy prey for the vultures in every city. Many have not completed their education and have no job training—not even the experience of a paper route. They know no one outside Junior Village. Many I knew were quickly institutionalized again—only this time it was the pen."

The hope is that the halfway house will give the boys support while they grow in "at-homeness" in the world outside an institution. As someone said, the Peace Corps and other organizations have intensive orientation programs for its people entering new situations, and these are young people selected in part on the basis of their emotional security. The Junior Village child, making the much more radical transition from the confines of a shelter where all decisions have been made for him, is given no help. The halfway house is planning its program to help these youngsters experience their own individuality, and give them an opportunity for growth and independence through job training, tutoring, and counseling. Initially, four boys aged sixteen to eighteen will live in the halfway house, which will be supervised by an older couple.

Another halfway house for girls is already under way. The girls will learn a few things the boys will not, for they are already learning about decorating and how to cook and make a home. The older supervisory couple in this house is twenty-seven year old Jim Alrutz of the Covenant Community and his young bride, Neen.

The down payment for a third house has already been donated, and as soon as there is a supporting couple another house will be bought and its young tenants found. Residence in the houses will probably be limited to a year, though this may not prove time enough to equip these teen-agers for responsible living. As they are able to leave, another Junior Village child will move in.

Out of the Home Rehabilitation Groups came the "Hope and a Home Plan," in which the Restoration Corps was participating. In the many-faceted story which is FLOC, there are many places to pause, if space made it possible, but perhaps none with so deep a meaning as the "Hope and a Home" program. It was based on the indisputable fact that a housing shortage for low-income families was swelling the population of Junior Village. The plan was three-fold: (1) To purchase or rent homes for Junior Village families, (2) to give rent subsidies as long as needed, and (3) to provide each reunited family with supporting friendships. The third seemed essential, because usually eviction had been the last in a series of disasters to hit a family. The Welfare Department agreed to help with the selection of families and to put FLOC in touch with them.

In February, 1966, FLOC bought its first house and rented another. Two families, one with six children, the other with eight, moved in. Before the year was over, FLOC was working with nine families, including sixty-seven children. One was a family of teen-agers whose mother had recently died and whose father was unable to care for them. Bob McIntire, one of the supporting friends, said, "Their world changes so fast. Years go by in a week, and what we would consider major changes in our life situation, they take in stride."

We had known that these families would need more than a house, but we did not know the extent of the help they would need.

Some of the children were potential delinquents, and four of the fathers turned out to be chronic drinkers, whose jobs were always in jeopardy.

Over those first months FLOC supporting friends learned something of what it is like for the third of the nation's population who are poor. One mission group prepared a shopping list and two weeks of menus that would feed a family of four on $45.78. During Lent members of the FLOC mission tried to use the menu in their own households, but very few could keep that kind of discipline, and as one supporting family said, "Even if I did, it would not mean much because my FLOC family can spend only half that much for food."

Most supporting friends visited with their families once a week. "If we had more time," said one, "I think it would make a difference. As it is, we have just been lucky to be available in crises." Then, reflecting on that, she added, "Maybe it wasn't luck, maybe we have all the time we need." When one family was being harassed by Welfare investigators, Bernice Nelson happened to call on the telephone. One investigator had been sitting on the couch making notes while the other had the mother open closets and bureau drawers and take out items for his inspection. For an hour and a half he had asked hundreds of grilling questions. They included, "Where did the telephone come from? Who is Bernice Nelson? Does she need the phone? Does she make calls on you? Does she own a car? Where did she purchase this item? How much did she pay? Who is 'Terry Flood' listed in this directory?" On and on the questions went. When Bernice called and discovered what was happening, she called the Welfare office. A clerk said innocently, "It must be a mistake. Investigators are told to leave FLOC families alone."

A FLOC friend was also on hand when a sixteen year old boy came home and told his mother that he had simply been walking on the street when the police had picked him up and had taken him to the station where they pushed him around, shoved him against a wall, and swore at him. Bobbie Barrett went with the mother and her son to the station and stood silently, supporting them by her presence, because she was white and they were Negro, and in that police station this mattered. Somehow it happened also that they were on hand at points of despair and discouragement within the families. "We never visit our family without calling first on the telephone," said Joe Clark, "but that night Janice and I were out driving and we said, 'Let's drop by.' They invited us in. There was no formality. They were sitting at the kitchen table and they said, 'Sit here with us. We have things we must tell you.' "

They made mistakes along the way, and there were halting places in relationships, but the Junior Village families had the capacity to forgive them and to move closer again. Dorothy Spencer said, "Sometimes we suggest what they are not ready for, and they back up and shut the door. Then we have to wait until they open the door. Sometimes they will suggest themselves what we suggested, but it will be later on." Another member said, "Most of us are truly amateurs. We can't plot it out. Every situation is a brand new one. The only thing we have to learn from is the experience of each other."

They did draw encouragement from each other, and this was strength to continue, but at one point it seemed that every family was in difficulty—crisis came upon crisis, and they felt themselves overwhelmed by what was overwhelming the families. In their discouragement they decided to ask the help of a Baltimore psychologist who had expressed an interest in FLOC and who had worked with the poor. He met with the supporting families for three Monday nights. They were strange nights of dialogue during which they learned some things they needed to know. Dr. R would say to them, "FLOC has answered a call, but it hasn't evolved a plan. You have to cut out a pattern and at some point say, 'That's it. We quit.' " As he stressed over and over the importance of setting limits on what they would do, they began to know in each other's responses that they had no limits. "Look," said one person, "FLOC can set limits, if it wants, but I can't. These people have become my friends. You don't decide ahead of time when you are going to quit on your friend. You can't say, 'When your husband loses his job again, I'm through,' or 'When you reach this point of adequacy, I have other things to do.' "

Bob McIntire said, "Giving too much to the families we are working with and making them feel indebted and resentful is a danger, if we are not free to accept what they have to offer us in return. The professional social worker may have to keep the relationship in balance by giving less, but the Christian is free to give all of himself because he is also free to accept everything the other person is prepared to offer."

Dr. R pointed out that the Welfare Department would probably give them the cases that had the greatest possibility of failure and keep for their own annual report those that had the best chance of success. His recommendation was that they look at their families and not continue working with those who were not obviously promising.

Few of them had "promising" families. One person said, "We want to learn what we can, but we also want God to create in us the capacity to be a friend." Another said, "We believe that God can use us, and we believe the power of this God has no limits. We can't decide ahead of time what can and cannot be accomplished."

Another person said later, "I tried to picture myself walking in to Mrs. D's house and sitting down with her and saying, 'Look, your husband is a chronic drinker. That does not make you a very promising case.' Generations of deprivation had brought my FLOC family to the plight it was in. I was willing to wait as many generations to see change."

Another question that Dr. R put to the group again and again was, "Why are you here?" This was the vital question, for it helped them restate what they had been able to state so clearly in the early months of FLOC. "We are here because we are called by Christ to serve the poor and especially the children of Junior Village."

"Christ is at the center of FLOC," said one person. "This is the only thing we have going for us."

"Can we say, then," said Dr. R, "that we are all here for the same reason—because we are concerned with our fellow man?"

"Yes," came the answer, and then the "but." "But we think it may be a unique situation when a whole group of people are acting in the name of Christ."

"You don't expect," said Dr. R, "magic intervention? God is going to help only in terms of the skills you have?"

Around the table everyone nodded Yes. No one expected magic.

"Then it is agreed," said Dr. R, "that the job will not be easier."

"No, but also yes," came the answer, and then explanation after explanation.

"No, the job will not be easier, but yes, it will be easier. When God calls a man, he equips him. If this was not my faith, I would have quit before now."

"We understand that we cannot baptize reality, but part of the reality we see is Jesus Christ."

"We belong to a community, and one of the strongest things in our favor is that it participates with us."

"Junior Village is the failure of the professionals. We have to free ourselves from the traditions and standards that both the church and society impose. We have to be willing to learn what we can, but also be willing to follow Christ in this ministry."

When the sessions with the psychologist were over, the group felt that they had been helped in understanding their FLOC families better. Their own position had also been clarified. Dorothy Spencer summed it up this way, "Five times Dr. R asked us why we were doing this, and each time we reflected on it and each time we said, 'Christ is on mission to those families and we are along with Him.' It was so good for us. Dr. R did not know it, but he was recalling us to what we had lost sight of. We had known in the beginning that we did not do it alone, but we had become so bogged down in the problems that we had forgotten this and grown weary. Now we had again God's Word to us."

It seemed as though their sights were lifted. Lest they get too exuberant, Fred reminded them that the questions raised by the professional were vital to the life of FLOC. "We need," he said, "those who will challenge us and force us to meet them on their ground. We need the experience of doing this without surrendering our own assumptions, or we will retreat into 'piety.' " He reminded them that their task was to steer between a twofold threat: "one, of thinking that because we act in the name of Jesus Christ our efforts will be rewarded with success, apart from coping with the reality of the situation; the other of surrendering our faith that God is working with us, and depending entirely on what we can see and control, and fit together and make work."

They were aware enough of their own struggles to know that life-long patterns do not change without something new coming into the situation. That something "new" had to be more than a house, essential as a house is. It had to be the Gospel breaking into a man's life. Jesus had not said, "Go tell John, the poor have new houses." He had said, "Go tell John that the poor have good news preached to them."

FLOC needed to continue the work of finding homes for the children of Junior Village, but it needed also to search for structures and ways to call forth the gifts of those children and their parents, and help them become members of a community that is on the "immense journey" of becoming.

One of the groups invited parents of their FLOC families to become members of the mission groups. Two mothers responded. Other mission groups evolved a plan which gave every FLOC child a supporting friend. It seemed crucial that the children as well as the parents have a helping relationship. Sometimes they took all the children on outings together. One time they went to the zoo and another time to the White House. One Monday night a small group went to a bowling alley run by two discerning young men. Ten-year-old Jimmy, who was filled with hostility, began to throw the balls violently down the alley. He attracted the attention of the attendant when one ball leaped over two alleys. "Friend," the attendant said, "brutality doesn't get you any place on a bowling alley and it doesn't get you any place in society. I'm going to show you how to throw a ball gently and make it do what you want." When he turned away again, Jimmy went back to some wild and unsuccessful tosses of the ball, but when he thought no one was looking he gave it a gentle and straight throw, and down came the pins.

Not everyone they met in the course of their excursions was so helpful. Tom and Betty Deen took their whole family on a boat ride, and only discovered that their club was segregated when they lost their membership.

There were individual outings as well as group outings. Gordon took eight-year-old Jonathan to the airport and told him why insurance is taken out and taught him how to do it. They then found a flight number on a closed TV circuit indicating a plane was due, and went down to the gate to check it out, and then up to the deck to watch the planes take off and land. "I want him to have," said

Gordon, "a friendly mobility in the universe."

The next group project for the children is in the field of art. They will visit four art galleries with their FLOC friends and after each tour inspect the prints for sale. The children will know that when the tour of galleries is over, they can each return to buy a favorite print. They will then be helped to frame their pictures in the picture-framing studio of Jimilu Mason.

FLOC is now eighteen months old. The population in Junior Village, which was 910 when FLOC began, is down to 560. When FLOC began, the Welfare Department was talking of erecting new buildings for the children at the Village, so that they could have a recreation hall and more adequate quarters. Now the Department speaks of lowering the population to between 200 and 300 in the foreseeable future—"and to zero eventually." The addition of 33 staff workers to the child welfare division has made it possible to give more families the attention they need. Money and temporary housing and other kinds of assistance are helping prevent the breakup of families, and everywhere there is a spirit of hope.

Fred Taylor is teaching his second training course for prospective members of the FLOC mission. The entire class has the assignment of finding a home for one woman and her five children. Each week the class is also sent out by two's to do other assignments, which include interviews with both a slum landlord and a slum tenant, working out a budget for a family on public assistance, finding out what $10 will buy in a suburban supermarket and an inner-city grocery, attending a landlord-tenant court, and visiting Junior Village, employment agencies, real estate agents, and housing authorities. One of the purposes of the study is to acquaint the class with the life situation of the inner-city family and heighten consciousness of the problems and possibilities that exist for the urban poor. Part of the class time is used to report on the assignments and part for a study of the Book of Amos, for like the prophet Amos, Fred is calling his people to become involved with the poor of the city, especially the children and families who move in and out of the shadows of Junior Village. "FLOC," he told his class, "is willing to be a test case in the pragmatic laboratory of the secular world where nothing is convincing but results. Our hypothesis is that seemingly impossible things can be accomplished when followers of Christ deeply and imaginatively open themselves to His spirit and follow what they can understand of his revelation. For too long," he added, "we who have enough, and more, have isolated our existence from the world of those who have too little. FLOC's calling is to reverse this process—to help us be present to the Holy Spirit on one hand and the poor on the other." In his closing class came the prophetic warning, "If we wait and do not go, we may miss knowing what could be the greatest thrill of our lives. If we do go, we may make costly mistakes. We choose between deadening safety and a dangerous, but whole life."

Epilogue

Other calls are being given in the congregation. In the last year we have begun two major missions. "In Vietnam," wrote one author, "a small and gentle-faced people, caught between two armies, have become living torches."* For a long time we had shaken our heads over that terrible fact and wondered to ourselves, "What can anyone do?" And then one day we changed the question and asked, "What can we do?" At first we thought that we could establish with other churches "Communities of Care" to give to wounded Vietnamese children the medical help they could not receive in their own country. A number of our people have learned Vietnamese, and we are ready to receive the children, but now it seems they will not come. Many and conflicting reasons are given. The mission still exists, formed around the question, "What can we do?"

Another group has as its mission the establishing of a polycultural college, which will be a miniature world community, a meeting place for people with many perspectives and various religious backgrounds. The plan is for the college to have an international faculty and student body, with trustees representing many cultures. Bob McCan, who is the moderator of this mission, says of the

* Bernard Malamud, in "Speaking of Books," *New York Times Book Review* Mar. 26, 1967.

167

college, "There is a recognition in the philosophy and curriculum that religion is a vital part of life, and that to study world religion is to hold the key to the meaning of most world cultures. At the personal level, students will be encouraged to develop a life-style that includes retreat and contemplation as well as active engagements in the world. The philosophy will be to create an atmosphere in which 'identity' and 'community' can be developed. 'Who am I? What distinguishes my culture? How can I relate constructively to others?' The campus will be the living laboratory."

The proposed name for the school is Dag Hammarskjöld College in memory of the man who was vitally engaged in two worlds.

The capacity to hear a call and to respond grows in our people as we live in structures which point to the inward and the outward. Man does not come to wholeness without both movements, but because we are not whole, the reminder of this in our congregation increases for us the "dialogue of conflict." The action-oriented say, "The world is the arena of God's concern. The need is overpowering. Let's get on with it. This meditation, this silence business, taking a day for retreat—time to develop a quiet center, to ask questions—it's not for me. There's not that much time. The act is important." There are those who respond to this, "But not just any action. Action grows out of hearing the word of God. It is a particular action engaged in at a *kairos* moment—not action for action's sake."

The "dialogue of conflict" is heard again at the point of our fourth discipline,* "Be a vital contributing member of one of the confirmed groups, normally on corporate mission." These are hard words for some of us. They turn us away. We have little works we like to do in quiet corners. We want to avoid coming into a community in such a concrete way as this discipline suggests. To get bound up in a covenant with others might mean that we would have to surrender our sovereignty. "It is not even very efficient. And what about my individuality?"

It is not much comfort that exceptions to this discipline are made for any valid reason, and that an exception is always made

* See Elizabeth O'Connor, *Call to Commitment* (New York: Harper & Row, 1963), p. 34.

for anyone participating in a group which meets to deal concretely with individual mission in the office or in the home. The fact that this discipline remains as the norm, helping to describe the shape of this particular family, is disturbing to those who cannot come to grips with the corporate dimension of our life.

The fourth discipline has evoked as much feeling as any issue we have had before us—perhaps because it deals with the heart beat of this community. It is that which is central—not peripheral, which can stir us up. At one time we discussed the fourth discipline informally for several months and finally brought the matter before the whole congregation. The most persuasive arguments for dropping this discipline of membership came from "strong" and "busy" people, holding positions of leadership in the structures of the city. But when all the arguments were in we reaffirmed again the necessity of living out our lives in small groups on mission. We were never able to conclude that we could have a community in Christ by signing our names in a book, subscribing to the budget, and coming to church on Sundays. Over the years church has come to mean to us that special community in which there is accountability. It is possible to be in many kinds of relationship with the church, and this is all right, if it is not confirmed as discipleship. Discipleship involves us in a community of specific and accountable relationships with at least two or three meeting in his Name. It is a community in which strengths are discovered and weaknesses revealed—in which intimacy will be found, and hurt experienced, in which we endure the brother who is antagonistic to our own understanding and values. It is the community in which we are sustained, and it is the community in which we are betrayed. It is the community whose goal is defined by a Life that was for others.

It would be possible that a few might know this kind of community without any intentional structuring of it, but for most it would not happen, and when it did it would be as a light under a bushel. It would not be a demonstration project, pointing to a Kingdom that was coming. We may not always need evidence, but there are times when we do. I think that Fred Taylor spoke for some of us when he said that he was not offended when he picked up an issue of *Time* magazine with the words on its cover, "Is God Dead?" "I read it soberly," he said, "because from time to time, deep down in my soul, that very question has arisen, 'Is God dead?' Are we being fooled that there is really a living, loving personal God working to redeem what he has made? I can respond to those who having looked at the world and their own souls say, 'I cannot make that affirmation. There has to be evidence for it.' This is what the New Testament says—there has to be revelation, convincing revelation to which a person can respond and on the basis of seeing it can say, 'This makes sense. I believe.' I am grateful that at those times when my own spiritual despair about the reality of God has been great, I have been able to look and see evidence. Every single time I go out to Dayspring, every time I enter The Potter's House, the thought crosses my mind, 'Look what God has wrought.' Out of a community of ordinary, struggling people God has wrought something—the evidence stands out—independent of my subjective state. It says that this is auspicious evidence that the Living God is at work among us."

Those little mission groups, so full of our envies and jealousies, our loves and hates, our great belief and our great disbelief, are the ground on which we move "from the dialogue of conflict to the dialogue of reconciliation." Slowly we learn that the outward journey and the inward journey are inextricably bound together. Both engagements define our mission groups. Yolande described them with another word—"relationship." They are based, she says, on the covenant, "I will be with you. I welcome you to be with me. It is in your being with me that I come to know who I am and it is in our being together that it is possible to know who He is who has the power to change us both."

This was always how it happened. Tom and Betty Deen worked with a family they first met in the basement of a tenement, which was everything a slum dwelling is supposed to be. A year later this family had all their children with them, an adequate house, and more comfort than they had ever known, but the Deens were ready to call their mission a failure. The children were throwing chairs at the teachers, the parole officer had brought one child home for shoplifting. Mr. M drank and would turn the heat off before he went out and leave the family cold because he did not want heat wasted when he was not there. "We didn't know how to contend with the problems," said Tom. "We didn't know how to tread that narrow edge between being a friend and acting like a deputy sheriff. We decided not to try any more. We would lay down a set of standards and deliver with them an ultimatum." Then Mr. M called. He said that he was getting ready to desert his family—"I'm headed toward Georgia." He had done this twice in the past, for two-year periods. It wasn't new, but it frightened Tom. He realized how tremendously he cared and that he was listening to a man full of pressures, saying that he was through. "I don't need that family," said Mr. M. "Why should I be tied down?" Tom continued to listen with a sinking feeling growing in him, and then the tone of the conversation began to change. "You know, I'm not feeling so bad now." After another few minutes, "You know, it's good to have someone to talk to. When are you coming over again?"

Tom and Betty did go over a few days later, with reduced standards and a revised ultimatum. Only things were different now. In the relationship was an element of mutuality, an element of trust. The couple were able to fire back at them and tell them what they were doing wrong.

This father's drinking has almost stopped. The teachers are sending home good reports on the children. Mr. M calls quite frequently and always on Saturday when he is paid and his friends can more easily tempt him away from responsibilities.

For the Deens the change is as radical. Revelation has taken place. They had despaired of change in this family. They did not think that the gap between them would ever be bridged, and then it happened. In them is the exhilarating hope of the Gospel that makes men and women live their lives in a different way. A telephone conversation and a visit, and they had discovered that they did not have to be teachers. They could be learners. They had sought to lead, and had become open to following.

This is what we have discovered in all our missions. The help given turns out to be help received. We are learning that we do not have to change people. We simply have to be present to others as the people they are. And for ourselves, we do not need people to change us either. We simply need those who will be present to us as the people we are. This is how gifts are called forth. This is how engagement happens. The Holy Spirit is in a community of meeting, and in this community we find out who Jesus Christ is.

If we are to be people on that journey of becoming fully human we need to live in a community with its life structured for those essential engagements with the world within and the world without. Today there is not much evidence of any kind of community, and for the lack of it war is waged in our own hearts, and on our streets, and in our world.

Above and beneath and through all the calls sounded in our congregation is the call to build the Church, to build a community in which people are free to discover who they are, free to discover who others are, and free to discover who God is.

The Coffee House Church

1658 Columbia Road, N.W.   Washington, D.C.

A Celebration of Worship

MEDITATION OF MUSIC
PREPARATION FOR THE WORD
  Praise

Leader: Let us acknowledge and affirm that we gather as we live, in the Name of the Father, the Son, and the Holy Spirit.

Community: Let us worship and bow down. Let us kneel before the Lord our Maker, for He is our God, and we are the people of His Pasture, and the sheep of His hand.

Leader: God is the one who gives us our being.

Community: The Author of our life and our death. He is the Lord.

Leader: He who is the Lord is our Lord. There are no other lords before Him.

Community: Amen.

CONFESSION

Leader: We have been given life, but we have not lived. We have been called to freedom, but we have found the burden heavy, the anxiety painful, and have returned to our illusions about life, and our deceits about ourselves. Let us, therefore, acknowledge our continued denial of life and our need for that Power which is beyond our reach, yet ever-present to us.

Community: O Lord, we confess our slowness to see the good in our brothers and to see the evil in ourselves. We confess our blindness to the sufferings of others and our slowness to be taught by our own suffering. We confess our failure to apply to ourselves the standards of conduct we demand of others. We confess

173

our complacency toward wrongs that do not touch us and our over-sensitiveness to those that do. We confess our hardness of heart toward our brother's faults and our readiness to make allowances for our own. We confess our unwillingness to believe that Thou hast called us to a small work, and our brothers to a great one.

Leader: We have known life to be good, but we have renounced our hope and murmured against our fate, abusing the world about us and all therein.

Community: Knowing that life is given to us only in the present, we desperately cling to our false images about the past and our imagined fantasies concerning the future. Knowing that we are received in being, we have not chosen to be. Knowing that we are mission, we have not elected to be called. O Lord, have mercy upon us. Amen.

SILENT CONFESSION
Absolution

Leader: "He who saves his life shall lose it, but he who loses his life for my sake shall find it."

Community: In dying to our false imaginations and vain strivings and centering our lives in that power beyond ourselves we are given new possibilities for living.

Leader: We are accepted by that which is greater than we.

Community: Which means that whatever we have done or will do, nothing can change the fact that we are received in this world, and that even now we can dare to be who we are.

Leader: We are valued as we are. Life is good as it is given. The future is open. And this is the one objective and everlasting truth—in Jesus Christ our sins are forgiven—may we receive this gift and live.

THE WORD
  The Written Word
  Spoken Meditation
  Silent Meditation
  The Word Shared
THE COMMITMENT

Leader: We take into ourselves the sustaining gift of life which bears with it the necessity to decide for or against a life of freedom and responsibility.

Community: We accept the gift of life and the responsibility to

and the So

ral religious communities)

74175